BALLET TECHNIQUE
Principles for the Horizontal Floor

BALLET TECHNIQUE

Principles for the Horizontal Floor

by
Marc Hertsens

Illustrations by
Jessica Lee

Published by
R&E PUBLISHERS
P.O. Box 2008
Saratoga, California 95070

Book Design and Type Setting
KASANDRA FOX - PERFECT PAGE
Santa Cruz, California

Cover Design by
CHRISTINA ANSBRO

LC 89-40238
ISBN 0-88247-839-7

LC 89-40238
ISBN 0-88247-839-7

To
Rene and Joske Van Beneden
and
All my students, past and present

I gratefully acknowledge the generous contributions of:

Suzanne Berry, Elizabeth Jones, Alex Peter Leith and Robert A. Kennedy for their help with the content of this book;

June Coha for the additional illustrations.

CONTENTS

INTRODUCTION

The art of ballet, like all the arts, evolved first from instinct, then through experience developed into a formal technique. This technique became the basis for artists to master their craft and expand their art. An art may be influenced by its geographic location. However, the technical essence of an art is universal. For the art of ballet, the universal principles are balance and mobility. Upon these principles all ballet technique is constructed. In addition to these principles, and to make technique functional, are the tools: the body and the floor.

Mobility and balance, dictated by the floor, divide the world into two opposing technical philosophies, both of them correct. The origin of this difference is architectural. In some parts of the world theaters were built — and still exist — with a "raked" stage (a tilted stage, constructed to slope from the back downward toward the audience). As the auditorium floor was horizontal, a raked stage enabled the audience to observe the whole person at any part of the stage.

For generations, dancers in Europe have performed on these raked surface stages and have adopted a technique that gives them balance and mobility. This technique, and that surface, have been accepted to the point that

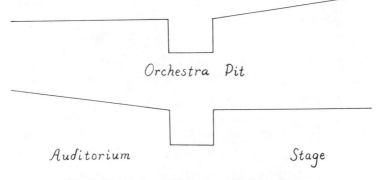

Orchestra Pit

Auditorium   Stage

Fig. 1. Comparison of Raked and Horizontal Stages.

class and rehearsal rooms were, and still are, constructed with an incline corresponding to the raked stage of the theater where the ballet company performed.

One could call this the "raked floor" technique. However, in the world of ballet it is known as the "Russian Technique."

Today's theater is built with a level stage, while the auditorium is raked for visibility, as shown in Figure 1.

It is the change to this horizontal dancing surface that calls for re-examination of the raked floor technique and adoption of the horizontal floor ballet technique. Once the basis of each of these techniques is understood, it is easy to appreciate the logical difference of placement and performance.

Currently, there is a continuous use of the Russian system by teachers, schools and ballet companies in areas where there will never be a raked stage, and while in no position to know, this author wonders whether today's teachers in Moscow, Leningrad, Paris or New York know the origin of their technical theory.

I do know that imitation of raked floor technique is rampant among those seduced by the success of the Russian technique, whether it applies to their performing surfaces or not. But in all the years I have observed teachers of the Russian system, I have never heard anyone mention the theory of a raked stage. Most teachers instruct their students from memory, without explaining the basis of their theory. They rely on their many years of repetitious training and recollection of the familiar silhouette of a position.

It is this knowledge that is presented in class as "technique," knowledge cut off from its original source. When technical questions do arise, there is no reference point, so the instructor invents an abstract explanation which can only cause confusion for the pupil.

This imprecision and abstraction can be eliminated if logic and purpose are incorporated into our teaching methods to produce a functional theory based on our current perfomance surfaces and the principles that allow their full use: floor, balance and mobility.

The horizontal floor gives us an opportunity to re-evaluate the steps and what they accomplish. Steps, as we see them today, still resemble the originals, even though they may not have been as sound and developed as today's versions. One has only to look at old gravure prints, pictures and even recent films to notice the development that has taken place over the years. At first the steps must have been only suggestions, gradually developing into the steps we know today. The steps and exercises described here have been selected for their typical use of a particular technical principle. For instance, the *tendu* exercise is used to describe the placement of the leg, the use of the floor by the foot, and the use of the pelvis in relation to the placement of the leg. The progression from *tendu* to *dégagé* is used to explain the transfer of effort from foot to groin, and the proper height placement of the leg in the *dégagé* position. I see no need to describe all the possible steps that utilize the *tendu-dégagé* technique. Rather, the principles of typical functions are explained. The use of a principle can easily be understood and practiced for all steps deriving from the same principle. It is assumed the reader will bear in mind that these techniques work *only* on a horizontal floor.

There are books and dictionaries that explain the construction of steps and give directional information for arms and legs. Therefore, instead of describing in detail the construction of each step, this book will discuss the principles that encompass the characteristics and practical functions underlying *all* steps. It is hoped that teachers will be reassured and aided in their efforts to improve their teaching, and that students will find clearer information than has been available up to now.

In the vocabulary of ballet there are basic and advanced steps, but there does not exist a basic or advanced technique. Technical theories remain what they are, the same for the beginner as for the professional dancer. Regardless of the difficulty of the step, the principle for correct execution applies. There are techniques of balance, *port de bras*, with their momentum-creating trajectories, horizontal and vertical mobility, the use of the leg and foot as one, and with their articulation, and the use of the floor. These techniques remain the only theories applicable to a particular function. But is *technique* that presents the step, and without appropriate technique, there is no recognition of correct presentation.

TECHNIQUE

THE UNIVERSAL POINT

The aim of technique is to achieve perfection in two areas: perfection of balance and perfection of mobility. In ballet, dancing by instinct, imitation or chance is unacceptable. To be technically secure is to be able to repeat movements correctly and at will, and to be able to master obstacles as they arise. Technical confidence is an absolute requirement for class or performance. There cannot be any guessing, contradicting or improvising. There is nothing abstract about ballet technique. It is, in fact, based on a set of principles which, when understood and applied, lead to technical proficiency, and to new clarity in teaching. Teaching should not only be showing "how to do it," but explaining why it is done as it is, so that the student can receive complete instruction.

Unfortunately, only rarely are teachers of ballet properly gounded in technique. The lack of a clear theoretical base has even led to the application of unsuitable principles. Yet, when the ballet vocabulary is properly established in the body, one can begin to find freedom, spontaneity and joy in performing ballet without apprehension. Only then is created the illusion that makes ballet dancing appear to be a natural function of the body.

In learning ballet technique, one works with each step and position separately. At the same time, each step and position must be practiced with consistent application of the principles pertaining to it, no matter what its character, whether horizontal, vertical or revolving. The character of a step is the intent of the step and its technical structure.

The intent of a step may be to remain in place, be circular *à terre* or *en l'air*, in the lower or middle or upper level. All steps, regardless of their technical components and actions, have balance as their common base. As for mobility, certain steps depend on energy created either by one leg, both legs or by the *port de bras*. Understanding the intent of a step provides one with the technical components derived from the principles pertinent to the purpose of the step. When the rules and logic are clearly stated, instructions become clear and purposeful, and technically consistent for all steps based on that particular principle. The two main principles applicable to all steps and mobility, relevant to the horizontal floor are:

1 - **All control originates from the back.**

2 - **Energy is applied always by pushing, never by pulling. (With the exception of *retiré* from 5th on point.)**

We are going to use these principles to re-evaluate the techniques of the ballet vocabulary. The source of all body control, the reference point for balance and mobility, is located at what

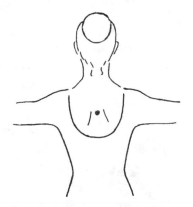

Fig. 2. Location of the Universal Point.

I call the Universal Point. This is shown in Figure 2.

The Universal Point is active even when the dancer is immobile. The action of the Universal Point is a constant slight forward pressure. This pressure serves to prevent the body from leaning backwards. The forward pressure should not be so strong as to cause one to bend or lean forward.

The Universal Point is not only the reference point for placement; it is also the point from which one controls the *port de bras* and balance. The proper arm placement in any position must include the opening or spreading of the shoulder blades, exposing the Universal Point, which is located where the vertical direction of the spine intersects the horizontal direction of the shoulder blades and arms in 2nd position. Thus it is the center for guidance and control, leading to natural and dependable balance and mobility. Since the arms never extend beyond the range of peripheral vision, the shoulders do not close during the *port de bras*.

The major difference in the techniques for horizontal and raked floor surfaces is in the use of the Universal Point. The raked floor technique requires control and lift from the front, pushing the Universal Point backward, while the horizontal floor technique requires control and lift from the back, pushing the Universal Point forward. Dancers using the raked floor technique on a horizontal surface will tend to fall backward when on balance or during *pirouettes.* The backward directed control prevents the dancer easy or comfortable forward progress. The legs are forward directed, while the torso is backward directed. This contradiction of direction will arrest the dancer's forward progress. Exercising the horizontal floor technique on the raked surface, a dancer will lose balance by falling forward. All forward progress is accelerated and becomes uncontrollable. The placement of the Universal Point is the operating difference between the two techniques, and the central principal of both.

BALANCE

There are two kinds of balance, vertical and horizontal. The Universal Point determines where the body weight shall be. When the Universal Point is aligned with the balance point, one is in the vertical position. The vertical balance position is created by a slight forward pressure from the Universal Point and by a lift from the spine, the neck and the back of the head. The chin should remain in the normal position. If the chin is lifted, the front becomes exposed and pushes the Universal Point backward. Another sign of lifting from the front is a pronounced edge of the ribcage. Once the Universal Point departs from the vertical alignment, one is in the horizontal position. The gesture leg, 4th *tendu* back, rises off the floor and becomes one with the torso, and as such, counterbalances the torso, using the pelvic joint of the support leg as the pivotal point.

Conversely, the raked floor technique demands that both the upper and lower part of the body direct the energy flow backward.

The function of all placements is to provide proper alignment for balance and to avoid distortion of the required position. (Never yield placement for the exercise.)

There exists a contrary purpose in the placement and flow of energy of the upper and lower body. The Universal Point controls the arms and chest through the frontal face of the shoulders in a back-to-front energy flow. This flow is constant, and that is the very reason why the arms are never placed beyond the peripheral eyesight.

The lower body is controlled through the turn-out of the legs, from groin, pubic bone and the cheeks of the seat, with the energy flow from front-to-back.

Figure 3 shows a simple device to develop and experience the backlift and true vertical balance for the horizontal floor technique.

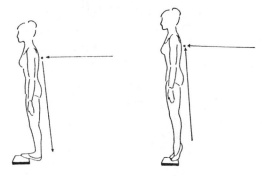

Fig. 3. Balance, Placement and Exercise.

Find a block of wood 1-1/4 to 1-1/2 inches high, depending on the length of the foot and the flexibility of the Achilles tendon. Place the balls of the feet on the edge of the block; keep the heels on the floor. Stand up straight, raise the heels and place yourself on half-toe on the block. If you rise straight up, you will fall backward. To counteract this and remain on balance, apply a straight forward pressure from the Universal Point, keeping the back surface still and generating the lift from the heels. The dancer should feel the whole back rise from the heel, lifting the back of the head so that the weight is evenly placed over the balls of the feet or the toes. The same technique applies when coming down.

Once you understand and experience the feel of the placement, you no longer need the block; you can simply practice the *relevé* and placement on the floor. If you lose your balance, place your feet on the block again and lift (*relevé*) from the heels. Do not pull up from the front of the foot or toes. Find your balance and keep the body still. Standing on the balls of the feet, with relaxed toes, maintain control of the placement through the entire back.

Start a series of slow ups and downs (*relevés*). Remember: keep the toes relaxed. This exercise can be practiced on half-toe or toe. The technique is reliable and will allow you to achieve vertical balance without changing the placement.

At first, the student will often attempt to do the *relevé* too fast, with the result that energy comes from the toe and the front of the foot, rather than from the heel. This anticipation produces a *relevé* which is too fast to allow placing the weight over the balancing point. It will lift the front, throwing the weight backward.

Vertical Balance

The vertical position is the everyday upright stance we employ. Our common mobility is walking, and we are virtuosos at it. No conscious effort is made to create balance and mobility simultaneously — until challenged. It is then, having to balance and initiate mobility on request, that our intuition becomes confused.

When the dancer is in an upright position, with the weight balanced on one or both legs (either on flat, half-toe or toe), the balance is guided through the whole back surface with a light forward pressure from the Universal Point. The spine and its muscular system are designed to support the torso. If our effort is in harmony with the natural structure, the beauty is that balance works naturally instead of artificially. At first the body will instinctively reject this position. But persistent discipline, and learning to discount the doubts that arise will re-establish perfect balance. It feels glorious to be on balance — safe, relaxed and available for any technical requirement

Horizontal Balance

All horizontal positions are characterized by counterbalancing the torso with the back leg. This placement starts with the 4th *tendu* back. Slight as the distance of the *tendu* is from the vertical position, the torso has to move forward to align itself with the back leg. The distance of the gesture leg can increase from *tendu* to *dégagé, grand battement,* etc. The torso remains aligned with the leg. It is the height of the working leg that determines the degree of counter-balance. The torso never takes the initiative in the counterbalance. Although the torso and gesture leg are in horizontal position, the second or support leg remains strictly in the vertical position. A common error is to freeze the horizontally placed body to the support leg (see Instinct). The torso must be able to move on top of the support leg without resistance from the groin.

This coordinated action must be strictly adhered to so that when changing balance position from horizontal to vertical, a dancer can keep balance or create momentum, without using the floor or a partner, and proceed to whatever action is desired. With placing the leg and torso in the correct horizontal position, the balance still comes from the support leg. Here, as with the vertical balance exercise, but without blocks, the lifting and lowering of the heel can be practiced. During this exercise one must be conscious of holding the leg and torso placement absolutely still, with only the heel moving up and down.

When executing the horizontal jump, one pushes away from the starting point, traveling *en l'air* horizontally and landing at a distant point, in horizontal balance or position. The rule of fixed horizontal placement and balance applies in mid-air and upon landing. After the jump is initiated and the front leg rises, the torso must transfer in mid-air from the support leg, forward over the landing leg, and must hold the counterbalance position upon landing.

It is this mid-air transfer of weight that enhances the momentum in the horizontal direction, and gives complete distance between the starting and landing points. Only when the support, or push-off, leg has been completely used to its fullest extension, and the weight allowed to reach its peak momentum, can one land in the correct horizontal-balanced position. If either of these two actions is skimped, the back, upon landing, will collapse and the dancer will stumble in the direction of the horizontal thrust.

The following are some variations on correct placement:

» The vertical balance rule applies in jumping forward, sideways or backward, landing in a vertical position on one or both legs.

» The horizontal balance rule applies to vertical or traveling jumps, landing in a horizontal position.

These principles pertain only to the horizontal floor. The slight forward pressure from the Universal Point, lifting from the back, counterbalance in the horizontal position, etc., are all unworkable on the raked stage.

CONTROL POINTS AND PRESSURE POINTS

A control point is a source of energy used to reinforce a directional effort and maintain placement. All control points participate in the pushing effect of the muscles. By contrast, pressure points are created with muscle contraction, causing cramps, preventing the muscles from functioning normally, and creating a negative energy, which acts in the reverse direction from the one desired. Pressure points and control points are almost invariably located opposite one another.

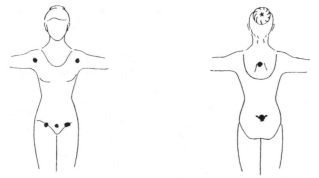

Fig. 4. Control Points.

The control points involved in placement and balance are the Universal Point, the shoulder face (the frontal area where the shoulder joins the chest), the groin and the lower spine. (Figure 4)

For example, all directional control of the arms and correct placement for balance comes from the Universal Point. If this flow is reversed by placing the arms beyond the peripheral vision, pressure points are created. The shoulder blades collapse inward toward the Universal Point, thus opening the shoulder face and revealing the chest, placing the back in a slight *cambré* position, negating all placement and balance.

Another pressure point is often created by lifting the back leg too high without counterbalance of the torso. If the torso remains rigidly upright when the leg has lifted as high as it can, further effort to raise it will create enormous pressure in the waist and small of the back.

Another common pressure point is found in the shoulders. Anxiety and uncertainty instinctively cause the shoulders to rise. It seems natural, when physically insecure, to react by raising the shoulders. This is a very difficult reaction to overcome, and a deliberate effort has to be made to rid the body of this reaction. The most successful exercise is the first *port de bras*. Place the arms in 5th *en bas*; raise the arms to 5th *en avant*; open the arms into 2nd, to close again into 5th *en bas*. In this exercise the shoulders remain in the normal position. While this exercise is not foolproof, it does provide the means to control the shoulders.

In addition to the common pressure points, there are pressure points peculiar to a particular individual. One has to be alert and observant to recognize such faults. There are as many variations in pressure points as there are students. The body gives a simple signal of a pressure point — discomfort and pain, which are reliable guides for correcting the flaw. To release the pressure of this negative energy, relax and allow the cramped muscles to elongate, and return to the correct position. Muscles work properly when used in their elongated state. Energy used in that manner will provide an even, relaxed performance.

ISOLATION WHILE BALANCING

Isolation is the technique of separating effort from balance, or moving one part of the body without affecting any other part. Isolation is the "diction" of ballet technique; without it, clarity and recognition of the steps are out of the question. Isolation requires discipline and restraint. It is what gives the dancer poise and composure. At first this is very difficult to achieve, even on flats. But one must be able to be mobile while on balance, without disturbing the balance. Economy of effort is essential to successful isolation.

Isolation is also the test of successful placement. Placement is the proper posture for the step in which one is engaged. In an exercise where isolation is important, the effort exerted should be confined to the working joint employed, so as to maintain a constant directional emphasis. The exercise should be done with an even flow of energy and without accentuation of the applied effort. The most common mistake is to emphasize the final direction at the end of the exercise. Giving an extra push off from the toes, or letting the effort spread beyond the working joint to affect the balance, defeats the purpose of the exercise. Applying the technique of balance and the technique of positional control makes isolation rather simple.

To remain in balance during the transition from horizontal to vertical position or *vice versa* is the most extreme isolation exercise. A total change of body and leg position employs the same technique either on toe, half-toe or flats. Again, the transfer of the body is initiated and controlled by the working leg. This transition must be understood, so that, when on vertical balance, the torso is aligned with the support leg. When the change to horizontal balance is initiated, the torso becomes one with the working leg.

With the torso controlled by the Universal Point, this delicate effort is timed from the inside of the working leg thigh; the torso follows the timing of the leg. This is the case in moving from vertical to horizontal, in the same way as moving from horizontal to vertical. There must be absolute immobility, and the entire movement should work as one, as the body pivots around the pelvic joint of the support leg, isolating the effort from the balance. It should be done only by pushing, never by pulling.

Mental Isolation

Theoretically, it is possible to practice ballet without mental isolation. But anyone who tries to do so will never become a professional dancer. The bridge between "me" (all the personal opinions, instincts, doubts and rapid succession reasoning and questioning) and "it" (the body) must be crossed. As long as the "me" does all the controlling, "it" won't work. The "me" must divorce itself from the pain and fatigue and practice objectivity in dealing with the body as a mechanism. The body as a finely-tuned instrument will only do as much as you ask it to do. By eliminating all interference and consistently applying technical principles, a dancer can develop an isolation of purpose and the ability to demand from the body all it has to give.

To apply mental isolation while practicing an exercise, one must divide one's attention between placement and the exercise. One must be objective about the body, treating it as an instrument, with respect, but without sentimentality. Isolate the mind from distractions, then consider the various technically required principles and effort. To achieve isolation of placement from the exercise takes time. Learning a step and remembering all the principles pertaining to that step is not all that difficult. It is performing with necessary economy, controlling and isolating the supportive part of the body from the working part of the body, with rapid diversity. I find this to be the only real difficulty in ballet. One must sense the correct placement, and — by "flashscanning" the whole body — work and still maintain the ability to order specific instructions and corrections instantly to any isolated part of the body.

Only with complete control over body, mind and instinct can one be a total dancer. For beginning ballet students, the most frequently used arm position is the 2nd position, at the *barre* or in the center. It is an excellent position for building up shoulder strength by keeping the position for an indefinite period of time. A variety of exercises can be practiced with the arms held in 2nd position, without reverberation in the isolated arms from any other part of the body.

Over the years, a dancer must learn total control and the ability to hold any part of the body still as the rest is in motion, a process I like to think of as "putting a placement in automatic." By "automatic," I mean assuming a position with the minimum attention necessary to monitor and adjust the placement. With placement isolated, the greatest amount of concentration can be devoted to the exercise.

INSTINCT

Among other things, technique is a sophisticated device for mastering instinct. There are two kinds of instinct of concern to us in ballet. Our aim is to cultivate one while restraining the other. The first I shall call "intuitive instinct." This appears as an innate comprehension of the art. Dancers in whom it is strong seem to have the knowledge before the practice, the answer before the question. Such people usually become the leaders, the innovators and the creative force of their profession. It is fortunate that we always seem to have enough of these talented people to keep our art alive. They are able, despite the lack of good technical teaching, to move correctly, even if they cannot always clearly formulate the technical reasons for what they do. These dancers are the ones we pay to see.

As ballet (unlike dancing in general) is artificial, and involves the body in unfamiliar actions, we are more concerned with the second kind of instinct, the "protective instinct. This is unexpected motion accompanying a given exercise, a reaction without conscious control. The cause of these unwanted movements is unconscious habit and automatic reaction to an exercise over which one has no control — usually an exercise just being learned or too demanding for the student.

Unconscious placement is invariably a habit connected with the feeling of comfort. The body feels comfortable in that incorrect placement, and it is therefore very difficult to sense the fault physically. A habit technically wrong does not automatically alert the body that it is functioning improperly.

In ballet training, we are more concerned with the second kind of instinct, the "protective instinct," unexpected motion accompanying a given exercise, a reaction without conscious control. It seems to be part of the body's response to the unfamiliar. Dancing in general is natural to us, but ballet is artificial and involves the body in unfamiliar actions. Conscious control protects technique from unconscious interference. It requires experience and physical sensitivity to recognize unconscious reactions. That recognition permits the appropriate corrective action to be taken.

Instinctive action has its roots in the self-protective mechanisms of the body; but during our early years we acquire a variety of habitual reactions, which are the first things our body does in situations of stress and danger, or in situations that are simply unfamiliar.

Conscious control of the self requires that we become aware of these reactions. Reason and analysis can be used to convince us of the right way to use the body in a particular situation. After that, we must be helped to overcome the physical confusion so often experienced when trying to exercise conscious control of movement. Then the protective instinct will remain to serve — more effectively in fact — its original purpose of protecting us from injury.

The habitual placement and the instinctive reaction never truly vanish; with each additional movement or demanding exercise, they emerge to be overcome anew in mastering the unfamiliar difficulty. At first, the "right" technical placement may feel "wrong." When the untested body first experiences the novelty and unusual motion of an exercise foreign to it, the posture and instinctive reaction may appear for the very first time.

Standing in first position is certainly harmless, yet beginners will raise the chin, throw out the chest and hug their bodies with their elbows. This is a posture of panic. The beginner must learn that the basic placement is the everyday, relaxed, assured and balanced stance.

The beginner has great difficulty mastering this principle. For example, one of the most astonishing reactions occurs frequently in the first attempts at *entrechats*. As the legs try desperately to cross and beat in mid-air, the hands imitate the very beats that the legs are attempting.

Correct technical practice develops a body memory and at the same time an awareness of the interference of instinctive reaction. [Once the correct placement or technique has been experienced, the body must be able to remember the feeling that accompanies correct execution. This may require only one attempt or many repetitions of an exercise until the body memory is developed. Once established in the body memory, the feeling should never be forgotten again.] The final result is economy and clarity, the very essence of technical competence.

Actually, dangerous steps in ballet do not exist. By the time a dancer reaches the stage of doing difficult steps, he or she will be familiar enough with ballet technique to be able to perform them safely, with conscious control.

Having observed dancers in a great many different schools and widely diverse places, I think I can safely say that instinctive reactions are the same for dancers everywhere. By observing a dancer's faults, it is possible to predict what the instinctive reaction will be. Knowledgeable teachers can tell instinct from technique; they can lead the student to substitute technical discipline (you do it as you know how to do it) for instinctive reaction (you do it without knowing how you do it).

DIRECTIONS AND LEVELS
OF DANCE

We have to be very clear about the frame of reference used to define the directions and levels of dance.

DIRECTIONS:

Two frames of reference are used. One is centered on the body (personal directions) and the other on the room (spatial directions). Various numerical systems have been used to standardize the directions. The most practical and widely used is the system of the theater.

These directions are frequently referred to in class and rehearsals. For clear communication, we need an agreed-upon terminology. Spatial directions generally refer to a horizontal plane. In spatial directions there are two cardinal

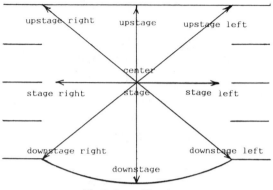

Fig. 5. Stage Directions.

directions and two diagonal. (See Figs. 5 and 6.) Although the shape of the space concerned may differ, center stage is always the point of intersection of all the spatial directions.

In the case of personal directions, there are three cardinal and four diagonal.

The 5th position *en haut* is up. The 2nd position of the arms is sideways and 5th *en bas* is down. Thus the directions are up and down, left and right and front and back. The diagonal location of the arms in *effacé* or *écarté* lies between the up and side placement. It is easier to find the placement of *écarté* and *effacé* if you place the arms on the rim of the sphere, at the diagonal point between 2nd position and 5th *en haut* or 5th *en bas*. Misplacement of these positions can be tested by returning the arms to second position. If this change of placement is accomplished without *épaulment*, the placement was correct. If *épaulment* is experienced, then the arms were placed beyond the second position and too far backwards. *Croisé* and *effacé* place the body at the intersection of two spatial diagonals: the personal front and extended leg in one diagonal, the arms or *port de bras* in the crossing diagonal.

The spatial directions are locked to the stage or practice room. Within this framework the body moves, carrying with it its own reference axis, the personal directions. When the personal front is facing downstage, all directions correspond; personal left is the same as stage left, and so on. But when the body begins to move, this may no longer be the case. An exercise can be performed with the personal front facing upstage, and the personal back downstage. Often in ballet variations there can be movement through space from upstage left to downstage right, with the personal front facing downstage right. For clear communication it is essential to understand these locations, their dimensions and diagonals.

It is not only at center stage that personal and spatial directions correspond. One can be placed at extreme stage right, with personal front

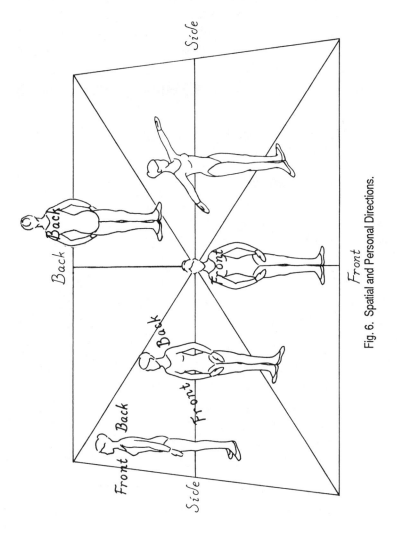

Fig. 6. Spatial and Personal Directions.

facing downstage right; here one is not actually located on the stage diagonal from stage right to upstage left. However, one's personal front, facing downstage right, is parallel to that diagonal. Constant awareness of the correct personal directions of the torso, the arms and the legs in relation to the spatial directions is vital.

LEVELS

There are three levels of dance. In the lower level all activities are from *demi-plié* down. The middle level is up from *demi-plié* into *relevé*, including *serré* on toe. The upper level involves all aerial activities.

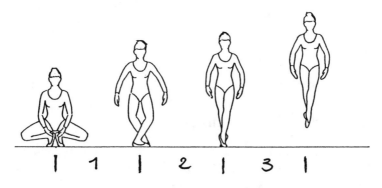

Fig. 7. The Three Levels of Dance.

Steps acquire their character and their intended purpose when direction is added to level. When introduced to a new step, a dancer must examine its character and function Full understanding of its purpose provides a more exact technical execution.

Consider whether the step is horizontal or vertical, and in what level. Is the step momentum-creating or primary? Momentum-creating steps are preparatory steps for the primary steps. Preparatory steps, such as *glissade, chassé, pas de bourrée en tournant, precipitation,* etc. Primary steps are *assemblé, grand jeté* and all steps of major demonstrative character. A dancer can determine what kind of step is being executed by exploring the following:

Horizontal and Vertical

A horizontal step starts from one point and arrives at another. A vertical step starts from and arrives at the same point.

The horizontal middle level involves *a pas de bourrée*; the horizontal higher level connects the *grand jeté* and the *pas de chat.*

The following three categories are an example of vertical movements:

1. vertical lower level - *Pliés*

2. vertical middle level - *pas de bourrée, relevé*

3.   vertical higher level - *entrechats, temps levé*

To transfer the weight from one leg onto the other horizontally, regardless of level, can only be achieved successfully with the use of the full length of both legs, transferring the weight from the support leg onto the arriving leg.

The *Glissade*

The *glissade* is perhaps the most obvious example of a misinterpreted step regarding level and directional dancing. It has been deteriorating as it has changed from a lower level horizontal step to an upper level vertical step. Instead of a lovely flowing, elongated movement it has become close to a small *grand jeté*, making the combination *glissade, grand jeté* redundant. The *glissade* is a momentum- creating step. The *grand jeté* is a primary step; it depends on the momentum created by the *glissade* to give it its full upper level horizontal character. One can be easily taken for the other if they are not executed according to their functional purpose.

THE ARMS

The mark of good dancing is precise, orderly, functional use of the arms. Although the end result of long, conscious arm technique practice seems unobtrusive, the contribution of the arms is equal to that of the legs. Functional arm technique is so harmonious with the legs that it belies their effort, resulting in a general impression is that the arms are merely decorative. Unfortunately, a great number of teachers and dancers adhere to that opinion.

First, we must realize the difference between class technique and choreography. In the classroom no liberties can be allowed; a dancer practices technique according to the rules. On stage one is performing choreography with all its liberties and interpretations. There a dancer executes ideas from a single point of view, that of the choreographer, and it is the choreographer's prerogative to decide what is right for each work.

The "decorative" arm, therefore, has its place choreographically, but that should not prevent accurate technical execution. Nothing is more enjoyable to me than to see the transition from decorative to functional during a performance. To achieve consistency of execution, the dancer's arms must be functional at all times — especially when the choreography has no other purpose but technical bravura, as in traditional variations. In that case, the correct working of the arms is essential. For example, thirty-two *fouettés* without full use of the arms is almost impossible. Many good dancers have tried and failed through lack of correct arm technique.

Male professional dancers are generally more exact than female dancers in the use of their arms. Perhaps all the circular exercises using the arms, such as *pirouette*, air turns, *manège, grand jeté,* etc., make him more reliant on the *port de bras* than she is. I believe that through *pas de deux* training, men use the whole muscle system of the upper torso according to its intended design. The lifting and supporting of the partner automatically makes the male dancer lock the arm to the torso, expand the shoulder blades and use the arms, shoulders and upper torso as one unit. The muscles which give the proper arm support are the same as those used to support and assist the partner. Although the working of the arms does not create the same amount of energy as that of the legs, the arms provide the added direction which enables the legs to achieve their fullest thrust. The arms must be trained to direct the weight of the torso so as to aid the effort of the legs. Since the torso has limited possibilities for creating mobility, arm technique is vital.

The basic purpose of arm technique is to provide balance and mobility. True, the legs capture the most attention in a performance. But no matter how well the legs work, without arm and shoulder technique the legs alone will never make the body move precisely through the balletic vocabulary. The legs generate the power to make the body move forward, back, up, sideways; yet any circular motion is effective only through the coordinated effort of the arms, as, for example, in *chainés*.

The shoulders are just as important as the arms. There is much less motion in the arms alone, and far more unison action with shoulders, arms and torso than is usually practiced. However, to decide which does what, one must examine the character of the step. Is the step in the domain of the legs or the arms? The lower half or the upper half? Once that assignment has been established, both arms and legs are responsible for creating their own energy and placement, to insure harmony and timing.

Regardless of the action, *port de bras* and placement always work the arm from shoulder end to elbow. Using the arms from the hand end will give a flailing impression, and it is useless for creating true momentum. The major control of placement and effort occurs from the inside of the elbow to the shoulder face. The area from elbow to hand follows, with little if any practical contribution.

An astonishing number of muscles in the upper torso are assigned to the support and working of the arms. The power of this massive muscle system can be harnessed to our purpose by locking the arm to the upper torso. In conjunction, the *port de bras* can move the weight off the torso. The main purpose in creating mobility when using the arms, is that a resistance, a sense of weight, should be created, projecting an opposing force against the direction of the arms. It is this self-generated resistance which will make the arms work meaningfully. All energy created by the arms must be transferred into the shoulders and torso.

The most revealing position to experience directional control and cooperation of the arms and legs is with the legs in 1st position and the arms in 2nd position. Both of these positions emphasize their traditional domination. The energy flow of the *port de bras* is from back to front; however, the turn-out of the legs and opening of the groin direct the energy in the pelvis from front to back. It is the very opposition of these energy flows that is employed to advantage in the *pirouette.*

Taking the 2nd position of the arms, start your control and awareness from the Universal Point. Open the shoulder blades and extend the arms in 2nd slightly ahead of the shoulders (on the rim of the sphere). Keeping the shoulders down, support the upper arms, preventing the elbow from dropping.

Shoulder, elbow and hand are aligned in a slightly downward direction, with the hands at the same level as the center of the chest and the Universal Point. The shoulder blades are spread,

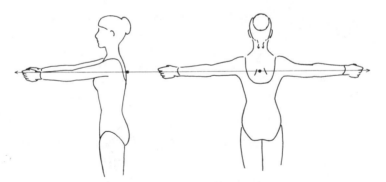

Fig 8. The Universal Point in Relation to 5th En Avant.

and the chest muscles contracted. In this position the arms and torso are united to work as one. All other arm positions adhere to the same principle, whether the arms are in 4th or 5th positions.

With the arms in 5th *en haut,* there should be a slow, elongated curve from waist to hand. Although there is a great deal of effort involved in the support of the arms, this effort should create no tension. There should always be the illusion of freedom and ease while performing the most controlled exercises.

When placing the arms in 5th *en avant,* one experiences the sensation of encircling. This is the correct sensation; it is experienced from both the inside and the outside of the arm. The inner circle starts from the center of the chest, with a firm lock at the inside of the shoulder, and runs along the inside of the arm, through the inside of the elbow and palm of the hand, to the tips of the fingers. This inner circle provides the direction and energy of the *port de* bras. The outer circle runs from the Universal Point forward toward the hands, supporting the front, back and undersides of the arms. The outer circle controls the arm placements. This division of function is essential for all *port de bras.* Keep in mind that one always pushes and never pulls.

As already noted, all the power and function of the arm originate at the shoulder; the weakest part of the arm is the hand, which has no practical function. The hand should be considered only as an extension of the arm. With the wrist firmly locked to the forearm, the hand functions as a gauge to line up with the inside of the elbow. Both the palm and the inside of the elbow face the same direction at all times.

The 2nd position is the simplest position in which to experience the hand and the inside of the elbow in the same directional placement. With the palm of the hand facing straight forward, it will take a slight lift from the upper arm and elbow to align the inside of the elbow with the inside of the palm of the hand.

It is essential to understand this lift when the arms are placed in 5th *en bas*. The same pressure as in 2nd position will push the elbow away from the body, open up the arm pits and again provide the correct alignment of the inside of the elbows with the palm of the hand. This lift is equal along the whole length of the arm and constantly supports every segment. According to the direction in which the arms travel, the energy for the *port de bras* must come from the pushing side — the inside.

For example, a standard exercise for *port de bras* practice is the lift from 5th *en bas* through 5th *en avant*, ending in 5th *en haut*. During the whole exercise, the effort is generated from the underside of the arm. During this exercise, and all *port de bras*, placement of the torso is not influenced by the arms. In this case, they work independently of the torso. The shoulder blades, however, remain open. The arms retain their curve; they do not contract in traveling from 5th *en bas*, through 5th *en avant*, to 5th *en haut*. Always keep the arms extended in a full curve away from the body.

During the *port de bras* from 5th *en haut* into 2nd position, the opening of the arms is activated by pushing outward from the inside of the arms, with counter resistance from the shoulder face to give weight to the arm and at the same time prevent the arm from working without control.

The 2nd position has three different arm placement (See Fig. 9).

> » First, when lowering the arms from 5th *en haut* into 2nd position, the *port de bras* ends with the upper arm in the correct 2nd position. The palms of the hands and the inside of the arms should face and be curved

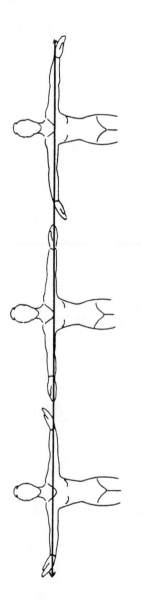

Fig. 9. The Three Second Positions.

slightly upward, and are placed slightly above the shoulders.

» Second, to place the arms and continue into the next 2nd position, rotate the whole arm from the shoulder, until the arms are slightly below the shoulders; the palm and the inside of the elbow should face front. This is the standard position and proper placement from which to proceed to 5th *en avant.*

» The third placement in 2nd position comes from the continuous rotation of the whole arm until the inside of the palm and the inside of the elbow face down. That is the correct placement to continue toward 5th *en bas* until the insides of the arms face each other. This rotation is done without lifting the elbow or shoulders. Keep a downward pressure on the shoulders.

All arm activity occurs in front of the body. This is a rule for all the *port de bras.* At no time are the arms placed beyond the shoulders. For technical reliability in the use of the arms, placement and trajectories must be constant. These placements and trajectories are simple and practical. Consequently, the sphere of the *port de bras* is is located in front of the body.

Here is an exercise to locate and establish the edge of the sphere of the *port de bras:*

Fig. 10-A. Exercise to Establish the Rim of the Sphere.

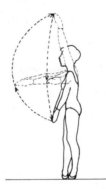

Fig. 10-B. Exercise to Establish Dome of Sphere.

For the rim of the sphere (Fig. 10-a):

» Face away from the mirror.

» Stand in 1st position with arms in 5th *en bas.*

» Look straight ahead at eye level.

» Make certain the eyes don't raise or lower during the exercise.

» Bring the arms forward from 5th position *en bas,* until the hands are visible at the periphery of your eyesight.

» Open and raise the arms sideways through 2nd position and up towards 5th *en haut,* so that they travel along the periphery of vision.

For the dome of the sphere (Fig. 10-b):

» With the arms at 5th *en bas,* raise both arms into 5th *en avant.*

» Then raise them into 5th *en haut.* Open arms into 2nd and continue into 5th *en bas.*

» By also reversing this pattern, one will have traveled through all the arm positions in ballet.

We have now established the sphere defining all arm positions and trajectories. Notice that when the arms travel from 5th *en bas* through 5th *en avant* into 5th *en haut* that the tips of the fingers do not touch, and each arm remains on its own side. While the arms work in harmony, both have their independent spheres and neither will trespass into the other's sphere. (Neither arm or leg ever crosses over into the domain of the opposing arm or leg.)

The most abused arm position is the *effacé*. It seems that many guess at, rather than know, the placement. The variations on this placement are staggering. To begin with, the placement of the torso is upright and the shoulders are in normal position for the basis of the *effacé*.

Efface Devant

The *effacé* placement is based on diagonals. In this instance, the personal front and the *tendu* are facing downstage right. The arms are parallel with the spatial diagonal from downstage left to upstage right. The arms in turn are placed from left up to right down, in an oblique angle.

Place the right leg in 4th position *tendu* front, both arms in 2nd position. Raise the left arm until placed between 2nd and 5th *en haut.*

The right arm lowers until placed between 2nd and 5th *en bas.* The head is turned to the left and raised, eyes centered and focused into the palm of the left hand. The head need not be inclined.

The common error is to extend the arms beyond the shoulders, reaching backward, attempting to align the arm with the spatial diagonal, thereby closing the shoulder blades and opening the shoulder face. The arms are no longer placed at the rim of the *port de bras* sphere and are out of functional control.

Efface Derriére:

Bring the right leg in 1st, place the left leg in 4th position *tendu* back. Keeping the arms in the same position as in *effacé devant*, turn the palm of the left hand away, but keep the eyes focused over the back of the hand. These arm placements do not vary, whether the leg is placed in *tendu*, *degagé* or high elevation in front or back. One must be able to execute *effacé* on toe with faultless balance.

Trajectories of the Arms

The sphere of the *port de bras* is in front of the body and shoulders. If you bear in mind that the personal front remains constant, it is easier to understand the theory of trajectory. Trajectory is the distance traveled by the arms from starting position to ending position, while the body remains stationary. The trajectories are as follows: from 2nd to 5th *en avant* is a horizontal trajectory; from 2nd to 5th *en haut* is an upward trajectory; from 2nd to 5th *en bas* is the downward trajectory. The trajectories become extended when rotation is added during the *port de bras*. For example:

- »   Place the arms in 2nd position.

- »   Close the right arm to 5th *en avant* (1).

- »   Close the left arm to 5th *en avant* (2).

- »   Open the left arm back into 2nd (3).

- »   Open the right arm to 2nd. (4).

- »   The arms have remained in front of the body and at the same level.

- »   Repeat the same exercise.

- »   Place the arms in 2nd position.

- »   Hold the right arm extended to stage right.

- »   Pivot 1/4 turn until personal front faces stage right. The right arm is now placed in 5th *en avant*. The left arm during the pivot close sinto 5th *en avant*, having traveled a 1/2 circle.

- »   Keep both arms in 5th *en avant* and pivot 1/4 turn, facing upstage.

» Keep both arms in place and pivot 1/4 turn, facing stage left.

» On the next 1/4 turn, leave the left arm extended to stage left; place personal front downstage and open the right arm to 2nd position, traveling a 1/2 circle to finish the exercise.

What at first was a simple exercise in arm trajectory has now become an enormously extended trajectory. During the pivoting action, the arms remain in front of the body, never leaving the sphere of the port de bras. The arms describe a full circular horizontal extended trajectory.

Spiral trajectories are also derived from the use of the *port de bras*. Here, as before, start with the arms in 4th: right arm in 5th *en avant*, left arm in 2nd. Raise the arms to 5th *en haut*; the right arm travels straight up in front of the body; the left arm closes in from 2nd to 5th *en haut*. Hold the position for counts 2 and 3 while revolving. On count 4, when facing front, open both arms in 2nd. The left arm has traveled a full half circle until facing stage right, and changes levels from middle level to high. In doing so, it describes a long half-circular upward spiral

(1) With both arms placed in 5th *en haut*, the rotation continues with the left arm describing a circular extended trajectory over the head, like a halo.

(2,3) Hold the arm position until again facing downstage, at which point open both arms at the same time in 2nd position (4).

This same spiral trajectory occurs when the *pirouette* is practiced with the arms placed in 5th *en bas*. The arms now travel in a downward spiral trajectory, describing a circular pattern around the lower body (skirting), which ends with the arms in 2nd. With the horizontal extended trajectory or the spiral trajectory the arms remain in front of the body during the *pirouette.*

These are the major directional trajectories that create the momentum for all rotary movements. Knowing the location of the sphere and its rim, and the location of all the trajectories within it, makes it simple to place the arms. There are no straight courses in the *port de bras*; They are either circular or spiral.

THE LEG

Correct use of the leg is the prime requirement for perfect execution. It is surprising how
simply the legs work, considering all the variations that can be created. The leg's basic functions are: to support itself, to support the weight
and to move the weight in an effortless manner.

When we analyze the working of the leg it
becomes clear that the pelvis, the thigh, the foot
and the floor all make their individual contributions toward a single purpose: technical function
for correct mobility.

The leg manipulates the weight in two
ways:

» Absorbing the weight (elongating the
muscles).

» Launching the weight (contracting
the muscles).

Weight is absorbed by going down into
demi or *grand plié* from the standing position or
from a jump. Weight is launched by coming up

from a *demi-plié* into either an upright, horizontal or circular movement.

These maneuvers can be successful only if the weight is placed over the balancing point, both on leaving and on arrival.

For the leg to work in the proper balletic manner, it must be repositioned from the normal everyday use. The turn-out is the indispensable placement that serves as a basis for the correct execution of all balletic steps and positions. The normal position of the leg is with the kneecap and foot facing front or slightly to the outside. For ballet, the proper placement is with the kneecaps and toes facing out to the side. This is a rotation of 90 degrees from the normal.

Placement of the leg, regardless of the source of energy, is guided by the whole length of the inside of the thigh, from groin to knee, with the turn-out originating from the groin. Once this artificial position has been mastered, the logic of the placement becomes clear. It must be kept in mind that, in turn-out position, the inside of the leg has become the front, the front has become the side and the outside of the leg is now the back.

Turn-out

The proper source of turn-out is at the hip joint. Rotating the whole leg as one, the ball at the top of the thigh-bone (femur) turns in its socket in the pelvis. The knee remains in line with the center toe; this alignment is maintained throughout all exercises and positions. Faulty placement here can have painful consequences. Trying to achieve turn-out by bracing the feet against the floor and forcing the turn-out from the feet could result in a wrenched knee.

With correct turn-out of both legs, the groin opens and the buttocks tighten. This opened groin and tightened seat allow an energy flow from front to back, in distinction to the energy flow of the arms, which is back to front. This opposition of energy flow is vitally important in *pirouettes* and in working the leg from 2nd to 4th position back.

The Straight Leg

There are two ways of straightening the leg: by pulling up the kneecap, thereby tightening the thigh and unifying the leg; or, by keeping the knee and thigh relaxed, pushing the back of the knee backwards. The relaxed knee and thigh are used for balance and for *pirouettes* on half-toe. The pulled-up kneecap is used when the leg functions as one. Many students use the tightening of the kneecap as a source of energy to raise the leg. This can only create painful cramps in the thigh, shaking of the leg and failure to attain any respectable height. The pulled-up kneecap is used on full toe. It would be impossible to dance on toe with a relaxed knee.

The leg has two sources of energy and support: the foot (with the floor acting as catalyst) and the groin. As long as the leg works within the *tendu* distance, whether the exercise is outgoing or incoming, all energy results from pressing and brushing the foot against the floor. As soon as the foot leaves the floor all energy for working the leg comes from the groin. A leg that supports no weight is in gesture position, and even though there may be contact with the floor (*tendu*), all effort to work the leg transfers to the groin.

For example, in *tendu* 4th front the leg and foot are completely extended, without weight on the floor; the leg is in gesture position. Because the floor no longer serves as catalyst, the leg must be activated from the groin. All the muscles that move the leg are in the groin, so this must be the source of all mobility of the gesture leg. This allows larger movements to take place at a faster speed.

There is a constant interplay of support and energy between the foot and the groin. As long as there is weight on the foot, the leg supports the body; but as soon as the leg enters the gesture position, the energy to support it comes from the groin. This principle is often ignored, resulting in indiscriminate counter-balancing, no matter where the leg is placed.

The working of the upper arm and the thigh is parallel in nature and serves the same purpose — in all positions, the upper arm places the arm as the thigh places the leg. The thigh determines position, speed and isolation. When necessary, the leg will be guided by the thigh independent of the torso. At times, the thigh will lock to the torso and thus become a source of functional energy.

The inside of the thigh also guides the placement of the leg, either straight or bent. The lower part of the leg, from knee to foot, will automatically follow the placement of the thigh. Only when the thigh is placed properly can the lower part function independently in isolation. This guiding of the leg from the thigh provides for perfect placement, economy of effort and large movements at *allegro* tempo.

The one technique in ballet that recurs continually is the transfer of the weight from one leg onto the other, using the full length of the leg, either to progress or to remain on balance. The simple act of walking illustrates this point to perfection. It is the transfer of the weight from the take-off point to the arrival point that dictates the technique of "pushing, not pulling." The different length of stride from walking to *grand jeté* does not alter the theory.

The principal of body adjustment to leg placement is constant for any exercise and any height of leg. There is a practical anatomical reason: the leg has a more flexible and independent up-and-down articulation at the front and side of the body than anatomy allows in the back. The counterbalance technique allows a greater range of movement for the leg behind the body, the direction of the leg determining the adjustment of pelvis and body.

THE FEET

When years of practice have brought some degree of proficiency, every dancer has to face that great eliminator — the foot. Many physical shortcomings can be tolerated and incorporated into an effective ballet machine. But shortcomings of the feet are the hardest to adapt.

It is encouraging if the foot is normally aligned with the shin. If it is sickled, not from the ankle but from the inside bone structure, there is simply nothing that will remedy that defect. Nevertheless, there are male dancers who have reached soloist status with a sickled foot. Their feet look bad, they are disturbing to the senses, but they have reached this level simply because they were male dancers. The poor female dancer with that defect would never have been accepted in a summer program. Toe work would have eliminated her instantly.

The ideal foot is short, wide and strong, with toes that are also short and rounded off, with the big toe, the second and third toes close to even length. Of course, an instep would be an advantage, but this kind of foot seldom has a natural instep. However, one can develop an instep, not as a claw, but with a true line and function.

"Point your toes!" That is the standard exhortation — and the worst possible advice for developing a correctly working foot. The foot is not pointed from the toes, but from the heel. The feet articulate from the heel pushing the instep out. The toes are functional only when on the floor; when off the floor, they serve to extend the line of the foot.

The natural action of the foot is rolling from heel to toe, with the toes remaining relaxed and pushing the weight into mobility (walking). This natural action of rolling the foot from heel to toe becomes a technique for raising and lowering the weight, for all steps. Keep in mind that all steps originate either from the *degagé* or *retiré* technique; the *degagé* technique being the brushing out and in from the foot and the *retiré* pushing up and down. Regardless of how the foot is used, all energy is derived from downward pressure against the floor.

Its simplest form, the rolling up and down technique, is the *relevé*; raising and lowering the heel without the toes leaving the floor. The *relevé* must start from the heel, leaving the toes relaxed. Usually, the *relevé* provides the maximum platform for support and is generally followed by balance. Balance, demonstrating the correct distribution of the weight, is not the responsibility of the toes.

When executing the *relevé*, one must remember that its purpose is to change the placement from one level to another. The weight must remain on the floor, not raise off the floor. The weight is only transferred from the whole foot to the ball of the foot and the toes. Attempting to eliminate the weight from the relevé will cause instability.

It is essential that the *relevé* be at a tempo that allows weight displacement, so the weight can be properly placed above the support leg, and balance assured. If the *relevé* is taken too quickly, it will be impossible to place the weight over the support leg: the weight will arrive late and off balance.

The rolling up and down technique applies not only to *relevé*, but to all exercises, whether in a vertical direction (returning to the starting point), or in a horizontal direction (arriving at a point other than the starting point). The best illustration for this foot technique is the *changement de pieds.* It is well-nigh impossible to launch the weight into a jump without full use of the foot. It takes conscious determination to utilize the full length of the foot in pushing the weight away. If this rolling up stops at the ball of the foot, the foot leaves the floor weakly; no height is attained and the foot flops about in mid-air. The toes must be used in the pushing off. When the whole foot is thus employed, the launching will be successful.

Conversely, landing from a jump without full use of the foot is painful. On landing, the foot should resist the weight until the heel is completely on the floor. This gives a soft landing. Without this total contact it is difficult for the weight to continue downward into *demi-plié*; re-launching the weight becomes impossible. Again using the *changement de pieds* as an example, jumping and landing without full use of the foot and the *demi-plié* will result in a bouncing effect, rather than a true jump.

The second technique used by the foot is the brushing action. As there is no articulation of the toes in the *dégagé* action, the foot moves as a unit, either forward, sideways or backward. However, the effort sequence remains the same: away from the starting position is from heel to toe; returning is from toe to heel. For this action to be successful, the foot must press against the floor to gain momentum and must retain contact with the floor until the foot is completely extended through the *tendu* position, either outward or inward

The last technique necessary to master for the foot is the pointed foot used as the principle technical effort when dancing on toe. The foot's pointing originates from the heel and the instep, locking and aligning the foot to the lower leg, to become as one, with the toes flexed inside the toeshoe box. With the toes flexed inside the box, becoming one with the box, the whole surface of the box can be placed on the floor, giving maximum contact and balance. Flexed toes will also keep the toebox intact, giving the foot better support. Pointed toes have the habit of hanging the foot in the toebox, causing the shank to break and creating bunion trouble after a very short time.

Mobility on toe does not come from the foot. It comes from the knee or the whole leg. Progression on toe is always through the *piqué* technique, *grand piqué* or *pas de bourrée*. The *piqué* character is subtly disguised in the *pas de bourrée* exercise, which is the only true traveling step, with alternate changing of the weight from one leg onto the other.

It is fairly easy to practice this transfer of the weight. Starting from 5th position *serré*, with the right foot in front, the weight is evenly divided between both feet. The back leg (left) flexes at the knee, lifting the foot off the floor and transferring the weight to the right foot. Return the pointed left foot to the floor by straightening the left leg. The instant the left foot contacts the floor, the weight is transferred from the right onto the left leg. The right knee contracts, raising the right foot off the floor. The right foot is returned to the floor by straightening the knee. Contacting the floor with a straight leg becomes a *piqué*. Transferring the weight from the left onto the right leg is the principle of progression. This transfer of the weight must be done on a thoroughly straight leg, with the weight on top of the leg, so that the support side of the pelvis remains in place. There is a tendency to let the pelvis sink toward the outside of the support leg. Together with the rapid alternation from one leg onto the other, the seat acquires a sideways wobble. This exercise develops stability, quick displacement of the weight and crisp contraction of the knee. After practicing *retirés* in place, mobility must be added to make the *pas de bourrée* complete.

Again, from 5th *serré*, right foot front, left back, the left knee contracts, lifting the foot off the floor and straightening the leg placing the foot slightly past the right foot instead of directly behind. The back of the left knee pushes the back of the right knee; this automatically bends the right knee and lifts the right foot off the floor. When straightening the right leg, the foot is placed slightly forward (progression). The left knee contracts to repeat the step. All placing of the feet is with a straight leg, so in fact the *pas de bourrée* is executed on straight leg *piqués*. At no time do the ankles relax or disconnect the feet from the lower part of the leg. The faster the *pas de bourrée*, the more likely the ankles are to relax as the foot reaches in the intended direction.

Regardless of the speed of the *bourrée*, never reach with the feet; keep the ankles locked, articulate from the knees and place the feet down with a straight leg. This constant alternate *piquéing* will prevent the body from bobbing up and down. If the head starts bobbing, re-examine the *piqué*. More than likely, the leg contacts the floor first with a bent knee, then straightens out. The head and the body should remain absolutely level and still. The exchange of the legs is from straight leg onto straight leg, keeping the level constant, presenting an even, level, gliding impression, the very intent of *pas de bourrée* on toe.

Rolling up and down, brushing, and using the pointed foot with flexed toes are the three functional actions of the foot.

A well-developed instep makes the alignment with the leg more direct and, of course, more desireable. An overly extended instep is just as bad as an underdeveloped one. There are two schools of thought concerning the alignment of the instep. One is that the ideal alignment of the foot and leg has the second toe in line with the center of the knee cap. The other advocates applying a great deal of pressure on the inside of the heel, so that the foot draws an outward sickle.

While there is no disputing the elegance of line created by the latter, it does have dangerous results. When continuously practiced, an outward sickle prevents a truly pointed foot when the leg is in gesture position. It weakens the ankle, and on half-toe or toe, the pressure on the inside of the heel tends to place all the weight on the big toe. This eliminates the support of alignment; the weight collapses the inside of the support foot. On toe, a lack of support is particularly harmful. With all the weight placed on the big toe, the foot is deprived of the large support platform of the shoe. The other toes cannot share the weight. This placement is very dangerous and impractical. Over a period of time it can actually disfigure the foot, and has done so in far too many dancers.

It is safer to control the foot with a slight pressure from the outside of the heel, simply to prevent the foot from collapsing at the outside of the ankle, making the foot more functional as a direct extension of the leg.

In working the foot, the instep and heel need equal attention. Because of its aesthetic contribution, the instep tends to receive preferential treatment, while the heel tends to be ignored. Outgoing exercises which favor the instep receive more attention than incoming exercises, which favor the heel and the back of the leg. In functional importance, the heel has far higher priority. The heel is practical. The instep is only visible when pushed out by the heel. In that position, on toe or half-toe, the foot is prepared to support weight.

In *promenade en dedans* or *en dehors*, it is the heel that initiates the directional energy, enhanced by the pelvis and the shoulder. Similarly, during the *pirouette*, the heel provides a major directional effort. All too often the foot does not revolve. Consequently, the leg does not turn, and the *pirouette* fails — all from lack of attention to the heel.

THE PELVIS

The pelvis provides for the legs what the shoulders provide for the arms — support and articulation. The arms can function from or as one with the shoulders. The legs have that same independence of, or unison with, the pelvis.

The normal pelvis position is horizontal, parallel to the shoulders. It is tempting to retain nature's design, and seemingly logical, but the working of the pelvis is a part of the artificial manipulation of the natural physical intent. In ballet there is no practical purpose served by holding the pelvis horizontal. It makes dancing difficult and contradictory. The Russian system advocates the horizontal pelvis, which I suspect has been unquestioningly accepted without consideration of truly functional technique for the pelvis.

Pelvic technique improves the turn-out and the independent working of the leg front and side, allowing complete mobility of the leg at any given time. It is very disturbing to witness a superb performance marred by a constantly turned in back leg. When a dancer is incapable of a simple *tendu* in 4th position back,with a perfectly turned out leg, or performs a *grand jeté* with a slightly bent knee compensating for the lack of turn-out, then it follows that the back attitude is also turned in, with the knee dropping below the foot.

One would expect that the principle "knee in direct line with groin and foot" would have been examined and the position corrected long ago.

Systems and teachers are notoriously resistant to questions regarding the function of the pelvis. Their attitude is generally, "Just keep it still and horizontal." If one persists in asking why, the answer is, "Do it, just do it."

Ask the advocates of the strict horizontal pelvis to perform *arabesque penché* or high *dévelopé à la second.* You will notice that the pelvis will automatically pivot backward, extending the leg into a perfectly turned out *arabesque* and, in the *dévelopé* leg, permitting height and balance.

Therein lies the contradiction: at times, the pelvis is unwittingly employed properly; at other times it is not. That cannot possibly be correct technique. There can be no opposing rules for the same principle.

The *épaulment*, with or without the use of the arms, is accepted as part of the *port de bras* technique. (*Épaulment* is a misnomer as the action involves the whole torso.) As with the shoulders, mobility of the pelvis is essential to allowing the greatest amount of maneuverability of and for the leg. Although that mobility is limited, it is necessary to use the pelvis to the fullest measure. The *épaulment* pivots from a central point, with the shoulders rotating equidistant from that center. It is the normal and accepted technical action of the shoulders. Keep in mind that the pelvis also moves in one piece, its pivoting point is above the support leg, lifting, lowering and opening backward on the side of the working leg.

If the *épaulment* is accepted and incorporated into the technique of ballet, why cannot the same acceptance and practice be extended to the pelvis? Truly, the proper technique of the pelvis enhances balance considerably and provides the perfect, constant turn-out of the gesture leg in all directions.

If at times the arms work independently from the shoulders and at times in unison, why is this principle not accepted for the leg and the pelvis?

Obviously, it is a principle which can no longer be ignored. The effect of correct pelvic technique is a straight supporting leg. When standing in 1st, and especially the 5th position, the legs are slightrly slanted inward from the pelvic cup to heels. Exercising *tendu* in 2nd or 4th, and keeping the pelvis horizontal, the slant will be retained in the support leg. What was a correctly placed pelvis at the start of the exercise has become an outward pushing pelvis (sitting in the hip) over the support leg. Raising the pelvis simultaneously when extending the leg in 4th *tendu* front or 2nd position, or raising and pivoting the pelvis backward when placing the leg in 4th *tendu* back, will automatically straighten the second leg, supporting the weight properly.

The gesture leg placed in 2nd position represents the dividing position of the independent working leg and the simultaneous working of the pelvis with the leg. All leg work from 4th front to 2nd, or from 2nd to 4th front, is independent of the pelvis. All leg work from 2nd to 4th back or from 4th back to 2nd is a simultaneous merging of pelvis and leg. Guided by the pelvis, the leg retains its position and turn-out during the rotation of the pelvis.

Tendu.

The actions and positions of the *tendu* are easy to understand. The *tendu* uses the full length of the leg, the foot extended to the fullest, without leaving the floor, and without placing weight on the foot. The leg is adjusted from the top (turn-out) as the pelvis guides correct leg placement. Each *tendu,* 4th front, 2nd or 4th back, differs from the others. The difference is the position of the pelvis: in 4th front it is slightly lifted; in 2nd it is fully lifted; in 4th back it is lifted and swung backward, extending the *tendu* leg. Besides having an identity of its own, the *tendu* is that part of the *degagé* and *grand battement* which generates momentum by pushing the foot down and brushing outwardly against the floor.

Tendu in 4th Front:

The pelvis remains under the shoulder but is slightly lifted while the leg is held back deliberately in its socket in the pelvis. The groin should remain closed so there can be no reaching out with the leg.

Tendu in 2nd:

Placing the leg in 2nd position *tendu* requires pelvic manipulation. During the brushing out of the foot, the pelvis on the working side simultaneously initiates a slight lift until the *tendu* is completed. This lift is articulated from the opposite side of the pelvis without moving sideways out of its original placement. The working leg will have a line straight to the floor. It can be raised by its own effort without adjustment from the body.

Placing the *tendu* in 2nd with a horizontal pelvis makes it impossible to raise the leg without adjustment of the body. With the raising of the pelvis, the leg can work independent of the torso in 2nd, as it can in 4th front. There is no possible way the leg can be raised off the floor from 2nd *tendu* into *dégagé* without this pelvic adjustment. When closing the leg back into 1st of 5th, the pelvis returns to its normal position.

There is a rather simple exercise for demonstrating this pelvic lift: Place yourself in your normal 2nd position at the *barre* and extend the outside leg into 2nd *tendu*. Hold this position and *cambre* toward the *barre*. Let the *tendu* leg freely adjust into the new placement. The pelvic lift will be there and the leg will be in the correct *tendu* position. From this *tendu,* lower the heel and distribute the weight equally on both feet: you have established the correct personal second position.

Tendu in 4th Back:

Placing the leg in 4th position *tendu* back again requires the assistance of the pelvis. The pelvis pivots back, slightly lifted, thereby becoming an extension of the leg. With the pelvis rotating in this manner, the leg is also given the opportunity to turn out correctly, with the knee facing sideways. This turn-out is dependable. As the leg returns to 1st, 5th or 2nd position, the pelvis simultaneously returns to the original position. The backward tilt of the pelvis applies to all back placements of the leg, regardless of height. For all positions in front and to the side, the pelvis remains parallel to the shoulders. For all positions beyond the 2nd, and to the back, the pelvis favors the working leg.

Dégagé

Instructions for proper *dégagé* placement are as numerous as ballet teachers. But in fact, it is very simple to place the *dégagé* correctly and to retain accuracy in repetition. The foot brushes the floor through the *tendu* position and leaves the floor. As long as the leg travels outward, the *dégagé* is still developing. But the instant the leg begins to rise, that point — the end of the leg's outward travel and the beginning of its rise — is precisely the *dégagé* position.

There is no question where that point is; the change of direction from out to up is very noticeable.

At this time it is appropriate to establish and emphasize the initiation of counterbalance.

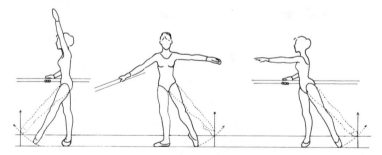

Fig. 11. The Dégagé Position.

It is in the 2nd position *tendu* or *dégagé* that the leg becomes one with the torso and they move as one, regardless of the height of the leg placement. As with the *tendu,* the *dégagé* leg works independently and without influence on the torso, when *dégagéing* forward and sideways. However, the *dégagé* backward has a very decided influence on the torso. It establishes unity between torso and leg, for all leg levels from *dégagé* up. The torso and leg are fixed at the *dégagé* height and work as one. The more the leg rises, the more the torso inclines and counterbalances forward — all the way into *penché arabesque.*

When raising the leg backwards, one experiences a slight pressure in the back of the waist, a pressure point. It is this pressure point that serves as the signal to judge the correct relationship of leg to torso. If the pressure is too strong, the back is too straight. If there is no pressure, the torso is either too far forward or the leg is not raised high enough.

The second leg:

The biggest difficulty of dancing on the raked surface is that not all directions are downstage (downhill). There is the upstage (uphill) direction as well. But the raked stage technique does not account for upstage direction, thus creating confusion, and troublesome execution.

It is established that ballet is "balance and mobility," and it is here in the technique of the second leg that the principle of mobility presents the proper method of dancing where the diversity of techniques for the horizontal vs. the raked stage are demonstrated.

If one were to separate the actions of the two legs, one would come to realize that one leg (the gesture leg) performs gestures while the other (the second leg) provides support and directional energy. They function independently of one another, with equal obligation to their respective technical responsibilities.

The action of the gesture leg should never interfere with that of the support leg; each must fill its special role in the exercise. A dancer must know the character of the steps in order to guide both legs in their assigned roles. One must be fully cognizant of the rapid and continuous exchanges of the legs and the basis for the role of each in each step: is it a gesture leg or second leg action? All too frequently, so much attention is paid to the role of the gesture leg that the functioning of the support leg, and its technical contributions, are overlooked.

The working leg has the advantage of being in view. It can be observed, corrected and enjoyed, leaving less conscious attention for the second leg. This divided attention is often unwittingly cultivated at the *barre*, where exercises are designed to practice the working leg, with the second leg receiving little if any action. But at the *barre*, exercises should be deliberately composed to include the support leg and discipline its technical responsibility. Considering the usually limited duty of the second leg (using its own length and projecting further than its own length), the lack of proper participation can easily be corrected to improve technical skill substantially.

The *tombé* is the simplest of exercises for the second leg and simultaneously provides a fine opportunity to discipline the gesture leg. The *tombé* (falling off balance) uses the full length of the second leg, with directional guidance, but without directional projection. With the dancer standing on the second leg, either on flat, half-toe or toe, the leg must remain absolutely straight during the *tombé*. The foot revolves at the support point, without displacement. During the *tombé*, it is the gesture leg that must be restrained; there can be no reaching out from the gesture leg.

An excellent exercise to demonstrate this technique is: *Relevé* on the left foot, extend the right leg in 4th front. *Tombé*. During the *tombé*, the torso must remain in line with the second leg, and the gesture leg must continue to be extended and held in place on the floor for the duration of the entire fall. If the gesture leg lowers and makes contact with the floor too soon, it will prevent use of the full length of the second leg. This will shorten working space of the second leg, forcing the foot to kick back beyond the support point. In this instance, as so often happens, it is the gesture leg which prevents correct and full use of the second leg.

During the *tombé*, the torso and support leg stay in line and work as one. The torso does not anticipate the direction of the *tombé*, nor does it hang back, opening the groin of the gesture leg. The gesture leg retains its angle relative to the torso. This *tombé* technique applies to *tombé* in 2nd and 4th back, as well. Once it has been mastered, one can progress to the *tombé* ending with the second leg arriving off the floor. Repeat the previous exercise: land and arrive with the second leg in *arabesque*. Again, the gesture leg should allow the second leg its full length and fall in the *tombé* direction, away from the starting point, without kickback.

The directional effort technique of the second leg is functionally more autonomous then when on balance or from *tombé*. The second leg can overrule the gesture leg by guiding or restricting the intended direction. However, the gesture leg must function correctly so the second leg can perform properly.

The principle of pushing the second leg to its full length can be practiced with the *temps lié*, either front, side or back. For example:

» 5th position right foot front.

» *tendu*, 4th front with the right foot.

» *demi-plié* with both legs.

Push in the forward direction with the left leg (second leg) placing the torso over the right leg, until the left leg is completely extended in 4th *tendu* back without leaving the starting point. After closing the left leg into 5th position, start anew with the left leg into *tendu* 4th position back. What was the second leg has now become the gesture leg, and after continuing with the *demi-plié* in 4th, the right leg (which was the gesture leg) now becomes the second leg. It is of this constant rapid exchange of the legs' roles that one must be continually aware. The concentration should remain on the second leg throughout this exercise and all those based on this principle.

During this exercise, the tendency is to reach out too far forward with the front leg, forcing the back leg to overextend and relinquish its position by being pulled away from its point of effort (starting point) and forward into the final position. Pulling cancels the character of the step.

One must keep in mind that the anatomic dimensions of arms and legs are the given dimensions upon which ballet technique is structured. These dimensions are constant, a precise measure of reliability, and respecting them assures dependable, correct technical execution.

The progression from *temps lié* is *chaseé* front, side or back. For example:

» 5th position right foot front.

» *Demi-plié* with both legs.

Again, push in the forward direction from the back leg. The front leg slides over the floor until the full length of the back leg has been used. Both legs straighten gradually during the exercise and are completely straight upon arriving in 4th position, *tendu* back. This *chaseé* exercise can be further developed by extending the back leg into *arabesque*, second or 4th back, with the second leg arriving at full height. The *chaseé* will be of slightly longer duration since the second leg will travel further away from the starting point.

A practical exercise to develop and experience the length of the second leg, becoming the traveling distance of gesture leg, is the introductory exercise for the *piqué*. Starting from 5th position, *demi-plié* with the back leg and extend the gesture leg in *tendu* front (*battement soutenu*). Push forward from the back leg. The foot of the gesture leg slides over the floor until arriving on the half-toe with the second leg extended in *arabesque*. The test is to keep the gesture leg sliding and not lose contact with the floor until the full length and effort of the second leg have been utilized.

Piqué:

The mathematical precision and symmetry of the *piqué* (arriving on balance) is fool-proof. When practiced correctly, it works without fail.

Start the exercise in 5th position, right foot front. *Demi-plié* on the left and *dégagé* the right leg into 4th front in horizontal position. The torso is in vertical position. Push forward with the left, while holding the right leg in position.

There should be no *relevé* from the push-off leg, and there should be no opening of the groin by the gesture leg. The angular relationship of the extended forward leg and the torso should remain constant. Simultaneously with the push-off, the torso follows the front leg, driven by a forward pushing from the Universal Point, keeping the torso in the correct angular relationship. The front leg lowers into the *piqué* with the same

Fig. 12. Piqué Forward.

descending trajectory as the back leg rises into the *arabesque*. The back leg, by pushing forward, will have traveled away from the starting point.

Using the impetus of the push-off, transfer the torso from the vertical support leg to the gesture leg and arrive simultaneously in the *piqué arabesque* with a horizontal leg. Keep the torso in line with the support leg even after it becomes the gesture leg for *piqué* or *tombé*. The *piqué* leg is placed on half-toe or toe; the back leg is placed simultaneously in *arabesque* at the ending of the *piqué*. Correct execution, which puts the weight toward the impact point, will invariably place the *piqué* on balance, whether on toe or on flats.

When practicing the *piqué* in 2nd or 4th back, the technical principle remains constant. The gesture leg must travel the full length of the second leg. Never return the gesture leg to or even toward the starting point. It will cause the dancer to trip. (However, on the raked stage this would be the proper technique.)

Arriving on balance from the *piqué* is best put to the test on toe. Considering that the *piqué* is a relatively safe step, even with the correct technique, it does become rather risky on toe. If the weight is not placed over the arrival point, the total surface of the toeshoe box will not make contact with the floor. It is the edge of the underside of the toebox that will make contact with the floor and, as a consequence, will slip away in the direction of the intended *piqué*.

Dancers will blame a slippery floor, never realizing it was their error.

Piqué on toe backward is at first unsettling, and justifiably so. Dancers learning it generally show a great reluctance: they will drop the backward extended leg prematurely, simply out of fear. The *piqué* backward requires discipline, determination and knowledge in order to overcome this fear. Indeed, one *can* be grievously injured, but if one is technically prepared, the chance of injury is very slight.

Bear in mind that the *piqué* leg must work as one with the foot; the ankle must be firmly locked so that the foot cannot buckle under the weight. A weak ankle or sickling inward will

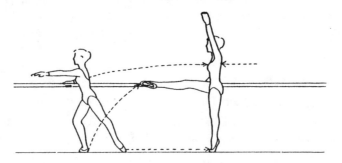

Fig. 13. Piqué Backward.

make the ankle collapse, and, as a result, severe injury may ensue.

This technique, using the full length of both legs with or without direction progression, applies to all steps based on this principle: *piqué, glissade, grand jeté,* etc. Of course, the second leg does not always end in an extended position. A step may be of a character in which the gesture leg rejoins the second leg (*assemblé*) or where the second leg joins the gesture leg (*briseé*). These technical principles are characteristic to the step and should be strictly adhered to so clarity and purpose are recognizable. The value of knowing the step cannot be stressed enough, for this equips both teacher and student with complete mastery of the step's composition.

THE KNEE

Although the knee is the link merging the thigh and lower leg, it should be considered as part of the thigh, becoming the logical assistant to the effort of the groin in retaining turn-out. Thus the knee is kept facing 2nd position at all times. Retaining the knee over the center toe becomes the source of energy that opens the groin and assists the groin in maintaining the turn-out.

When the thighs are only able to move in one piece, the surface from groin to knee is constantly pressed in the backward direction. Indeed, even when moving the leg in a forward direction, the backward pressure must be maintained simply to give weight and correct placement to the leg.

Isolating the working of the lower leg from the thigh is accomplished by relaxing the back or underside of the knee. The support of the leg comes from the groin, the placement comes from the thigh, and the free motion of the lower part of the leg can only be achieved by a relaxed knee. There is a tendency in early practice not to allow isolation of the lower part of the leg from the upper. Consequently, instead of the articulation of the knee, movement originates from the groin, with the leg moving as one piece. Most beginners have this problem with *rond de jambe en l'air*. It is therefore advisable to introduce and practice the *ballonné* exercise before attempting the *rond de jambe* exercise. It does not take too long before relaxation of the knee is understood. Depending on the character of the exercise, isolation of the lower part of the leg will allow the accent to be either inward or outward, away from the supporting leg.

To develop a feeling of merging the thigh with the lower part of the leg while the knee is bent, one can practice placing the leg from *retiré* position into the *attitude* front, side and back position. Since the *retiré* angle of the leg is the same as the *attitude* angle, the exercise requires that the leg remain in its position while the thigh controls placements. The height of the *attitude* placement must be such that in *attitude* front or 2nd, the knee is raised above the groin. When placing the leg in back *attitude*, the whole leg must be raised as one. All too frequently the leg is lifted from the foot, with a break at the knee, the leg forming a shallow "V" with the knee pointing down. The correct line of the back *attitude* is with the knee supported in line with groin and foot.

Another exercise for developing the feeling of merging the upper and lower part of the leg while the knee is bent is: *demi-plié* with both legs, then raise the heels as high as possible (*relevé*) while remaining in the *demi-plié* position. At first there will be some vibrating from the feet, but that is easily corrected by consciously taking the effort out of the feet and using them as normal *relevé* support. This exercise can also be practiced with one leg at a time. The most advanced use of this practice, of course, is *changement de pieds*, on toe. It is the controlling and articulating of the knee at the same time which is most challenging.

Of all the relatively weak parts of the body, the knee is where age and wear are first experienced. It is not as vulnerable as the ankle, yet, without ever suffering actual injury, knees will still let dancers know when time has run out. There does not seem to be any way to prevent or delay that sad process.

PIROUETTES

Successful execution of the *pirouette* is the chief ambition of young dancers. At any audition or class there will be somebody practicing pirouettes. They are a status symbol. Multiple *pirouettes* engender such deep respect that other shortcomings are — temporarily — overlooked.

Pirouettes may be executed in many positions. However, there are only two directions of rotation: *en dehors* and *en dedans* (outside and inside). Normally these directions cause very little confusion, but with the use of more advanced positions, misinterpretation may arise.

The *pirouette* is a compound exercise, in which several different techniques are combined for practical execution. The technique used for one particular *pirouette* is the same used for multiple repetitions of the same *pirouette*. The main effort for *pirouettes*, and all revolving steps, originates from the shoulders and the weight. Without the arms guiding, moving the weight in a circular path, even a simple *chainés* would be out of the question. Whenever a circular step or circular floor pattern (*manèges*), is required, the arms and shoulders induce the rotation.

Preparation

Preparation is usually misunderstood. The *pirouette* is created by pushing the weight through the requested placement. One must be clear whether weight or muscle power is used to generate the turn.

Launching the weight will give the experience and understanding of the power needed to revolve. If a circular step does not work, chances are that the arms, shoulders and foot are not functioning as they should. The *port de bras* may vary from one turn to the next, but the technique of working the weight circularly remains the same: connect effort (arms and legs) to the weight (body).

Whichever the direction or position of the *pirouette*, the *port de bras* preparation and trajectory are always *en dedans*. This simple formula applies to all *pirouettes*. It is very easy to remember!

In an *en dedans pirouette*, rotation of the upper torso is generated by the shoulder and arm moving inside. This effort is assisted by the working leg coming from the preparation pushing the groin and the inside of the thigh *en dedans*. In the *en dehors pirouette*, rotation is generated by the shoulder and arm from the opposite side of the working leg, which now assists the arm preparation by pushing the groin and inside of the thigh backward. The fact that the direction of the pirouette is indicated by the direction of the leg does not mean the major effort derives from that leg; the revolving effort remains with the arms and shoulders.

» *En dedans*: same shoulder, same leg.

» *En dehors*: opposite shoulder from leg.

The energy points and their unison effort are illustrated in the following exercise: Place the right leg into *retiré* and the arms in 2nd position. Commence an *en dedans promenade* with the momentum created from the incoming right shoulder, the incoming groin and the whole length of the inside of the right thigh. The initial progress originates from the inside of the support heel (right), with the turn-out dictating the stages the heel needs to travel and pivot the whole foot. Keep the toes relaxed. After the heel starts, the right shoulder and pelvis push the torso in conjunction with the heel's progress.

Note: This progression should never be reversed.

To initiate the progress from the torso followed by the heel creates a twisting effect. The heel should never leave the floor. It is smooth enough to take the weight off the heel and transfer it to the ball of the foot so that the heel is free to slide without losing contact with the floor.

After doing this exercise *en dedans*, practice it *en dehors*. Now it is the outside of the heel that initiates the progress. *Promenade*, with the inside of the gesture thigh and groin pushing backward, and the incoming shoulder pushing forward.

When this preliminary exercise of using the energy points is understood and experienced, one can progress into the *pirouette* itself.

The energy points during the *pirouette* are the inside of the shoulder and the inside thigh of the working leg. If the leg is not firmly locked at the groin with maximum turn-out, the connection merging the lower torso with the leg will be cancelled and the centrifugal force created by the weight of the leg will be lost.

The principal purpose of the *pirouette* is to revolve. Obvious as this seems, it still presents difficulties for many dancers. One must keep in mind that, after the preparation, the weight must be pushed along a circular path. The full use of the weight is imperative to enhance the power initiated by the preparation of the arms and legs. This directional effort must be divided between the preparation, balance, placement of the *pirouette* position, the trajectory and the rotation.

The preparation should not end at the placement; it is not only positional, but, in fact, mainly locomotive. The preparation should give full directional effort to the arms and legs past the placement and it is essential that the sequence of action, from preparation to place-ment, be accelerated into the speed of the *pirouette*. The dancer should not try to move from the preparatory position directly into the speed of the pirouette.

If the *relevé* is taken too fast, the weight will not displace itself at that speed, and whatever circular momentum was created will be dissipated. Moreover, if the *retiré* leg is pulled off the floor and an unsupported incoming arm swung into position, the unhappy result will be the folding of the arm and leg at the shoulder and groin, creating a lack of momentum.

Pirouette en Dehors

Here is a typical en dehors pirouette: In starting from 4th position *demi-plié*, right leg in back, 4th *port de bras* with the right arm in front, the following sequence of actions take place:

From 4th position *demi-plié*, without any extra dip into the *demi-plié*, push the weight onto the *relevé* position and balance. The balance must be placed first, before anything else, making sure that its lift and control come from the back. At this point, relax the toes. Active toes will push the weight off balance.

During the *relevé*, do not take weight off the floor; keep it firmly on the floor. While in the *demi-plié*, one experiences backward pressure inside the thigh, created by keeping the thigh's turn-out and place over the foot. This pressure is maintained from 4th *demi-plié* through the *retiré* position and the whole single or multiple *pirouette*

As soon as the back leg leaves the floor, the lower part of the leg remaining aligned, place the tip of the toes against the inside of the supporting knee. At the same time, the working knee and thigh push backward from the 2nd

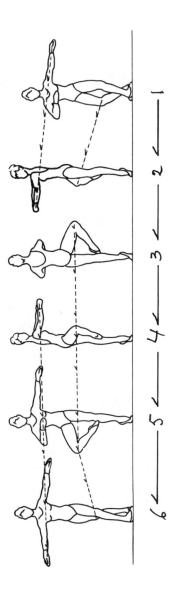

Fig. 14. Pirouette in Dehors.

position in the direction of the turn. This backward pressure of the knee and inside of the thigh causes full opening of the groin until, in locking, the leg merges with the lower torso. With leg and torso joined together as one, the thigh continuously pushes backward, taking the lower torso around. There is a tendency to initiate the rotation by the push of the working leg against the floor. This is a wrong source of rotational energy.

The working leg pushes the weight on balance, while the arms, shoulders and groin provide the rotational energy.

During the turn, the supporting foot must be allowed to rotate. Immobility of the foot is a frequent cause of unsuccessful *pirouettes*. However, it is alien for the foot to rotate. The instinctive reaction is to grab the floor with the toes or keep the foot still, preventing the turn. Yet this instinctive reluctance of the foot must be mastered.

One must deliberately relax the toes and prevent their grabbing the floor, while encouraging the heel to press along with the leg and body in the direction of the *pirouette*. Without this capability, multiple pirouettes are impossible.

To counteract the instinct successfully, the dancer must understand that balance placement is the everyday, relaxed, assured stance — a great advantage over the raked stage technique, with its artificial stance.

The chin and shoulders are at normal level, the chest and back in natural position, and a host of normal placements that generally taken for granted are retained.

These placements are as correct for everyday stance as they are for ballet technique. One need not be an experienced observer to notice when such natural placements are awkward. They are so natural as to be virtually self-correcting simply by checking the normality of placement. This self-corrective principle is of great value since it is so easy to recognize it in oneself and others. The dialogue for correction is understandable, the feeling is recognizable, and the faults are basic and obvious. The fundamental placement of all parts of the body is therefore a part of ballet placement. Regardless how sophisticated a position or exercise is, it will always be a part of normal stance and function, within the difficulty.

Since the normal stance is essential, parts of the body (primarily the legs) have to be restructured into a "normal" balletic stance. Once that stance is understood, it is easy to eliminate instinctive conflict with a suitable placement correction.

During the preparation for the *pirouette en dehors,* the legs are in 4th position — left front, right back — *demi-plié,* the arms are in 4th front, the right arm is front and the left in 2nd. Do not open the front arm or turn the palm down, and do not move the front arm between the *demi-plié* and the *relevé.* At the completion of the *relevé,* the left arm, including the hand, scoops with a circular motion into the 5th position *en avant.* Since the arms are locked at the shoulder, the scooping motion of the incoming arm forces the upper torso to rotate. The left arm will not be placed in 5th *en avant* until it has traveled a full half circle and is facing stage right.

At this point it catches up with the right arm, which is still and which, with the body, has traveled only a quarter turn. It is this "catching up" of the left arm with the right which accelerates the directional energy and, combined with the backward push of the working right leg, makes the turn effective.

After a three-quarter turn, the left arm has arrived at its starting/ending position; it remains there while the body continues a quarter turn and is facing front. The right arm simultaneously opens and travels the last half-turn, to end in 2nd position, and all motion stops. At the end of the turn, the working leg and foot are placed in 5th position back.

The *port de bras* has completed a three hundred and sixty degree horizontal trajectory and has passed from 4th front through 5th front and back through 4th front, to end in 2nd position. The energy created by the *port de bras* is accelerated during the preparation and into the speed of the *pirouette* maintained throughout the turn.

Pirouette en Dedans

For the inside *pirouette*, the motivating energy again comes from the arm and shoulder face and from the groin and leg, this time originating entirely from the same side. For the sake of variety, let us describe an inside *pirouette* with the arms placed in 5th *en haut*.

Start from 4th position *demi-plié*, right foot front, arms in 4th position with the left arm extended into 2nd position. As with the *en dehors pirouette*, the sequence of actions for the turn starts with the *relevé* and balance. The left leg pushes into *retiré*, the tip of the toes against the inside of the supporting leg and the knee opened in 2nd position. But instead of the backward momentum, in the *en dehors* turn, the pressure in *en dedans* is applied from the groin, using the full weight of the leg pushed in the direction of the turn. Again, do not stop the weight acceleration once the *retiré* position is reached.

Keep the momentum going by retaining the inside push from the arm, groin and thigh until the end of the turn. On the *relevé*, the arm lifts; the left arm, having traveled a half circle in an upward oblique trajectory until facing stage left, joins the right in 5th *en haut*. With the arms in 5th *en haut*, the left hand will trace a circular pattern. Remember that the hands are on the rim of vision and not directly over the head.

Because they are not placed on the axis of rotation, the circular pattern they trace serves to provide momentum until the turn is completed. At the end of the turn the arms open from 5th *en haut* into 2nd position and the left leg and foot close in 5th position front.

To often the *port de bras* preparation for *pirouettes* with arms in 5th or 4th *en haut* is incomplete. The incoming arm starts its preparation, but as it should be tracing the correct trajectory from 2nd to the *en haut* position up and forward of the head, the torso anticipates the completion of the *port de bras* and starts revolving prematurely. As a result, the arms never finish the preparation, arriving either straight above or beyond the head. In these positions, the arms cannot be locked at the shoulder and the shoulder blades collapse inward, cancelling the function of the Universal Point. All momentum has been lost.

When practicing the inside *pirouette* be careful not to fling the working leg through 2nd position before placing it in *retiré*.

That is not an *en dedans* turn; it is an *en dedans fouetté*. Many teachers and dancers mistake one for the other.

Fouetté

Without doubt, the height of achievement for all female dancers is thirty-two *fouettés* on toe. Regardless of a dancer's standing (corps de ballet, soloist or star), the thirty-two *fouettés* remain a classic challenge.

The difficulty of the *fouetté* is not found in the single turn, but in the repetition of the exercise. Many a dancer can execute one or a few *fouettés* without much difficulty, but relatively

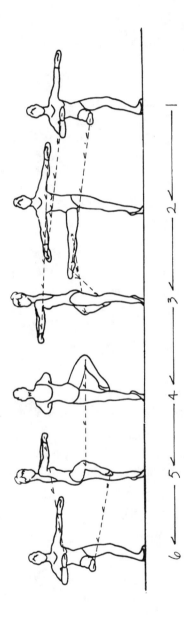

Fig. 15. Fouetté

few can surmount the challenge of consistent repetition.

Like the *pirouette*, the *fouetté* is a compound exercise, and all the contributing techniques have to be exact, or the thirty-two revolutions will never be mastered. The technical rule "Never sacrifice placement for the exercise" has never been more relevant than in the multiple *fouetté*. Regardless of the "wind-up," whether *pas de bourrée en tournant coupé* or double *pirouette coupé*, the preparation for *fouetté* begins from *demi-plié* on the left leg and 4th position *dégagé* front with the right leg, or *vice versa.*

If one were to divide the *fouetté* exercise into parts, there would be two major sections: preparation and revolution. As a rule, I have students practice the preparation without initiating the turn. It is, in fact, the repeated preparation between each turn that is the stumbling block for multiple *fouettés*.

The preparation: The left leg is in *demi-plié*, the right in *dégagé* fourth front; the arms are in 4th position with the right arm in front and the left arm in 2nd. That is the starting position for the preparation.

To start the *pirouette*, this opening of the right leg and arm are performed simultaneously and absolutely parallel to each other.

To complete the preparation, the right arm and leg open from 4th front into 2nd position at the same time, while the left leg simultaneously rises into *relevé*. The *relevé* is of the utmost importance, since the balance has to be maintained for the combined duration of preparation and *pirouette*. It is imperative that each part of the *fouetté* is allotted time for its full functional completion in order to achieve a successful exercise.

The *relevé* during the preparation must be allowed the time it needs for the arm and leg to open completely in 2nd position before the turn can commence. It takes time to *relevé* during the preparation on toe from *demi-plié* and to place the body on top of the support leg. If that time is not fully allotted, the rise will be incomplete and the torso will be unable to situate itself on top of the support leg; as a result, the support side of the pelvis will protrude sideways (sitting on the hip).

Also, because the right leg will not have had enough time to open completely in second, the *passé* takes place prematurely, commencing the turn and accelerating the rotation. If it is rushed from the very start, the exercise will be performed off balance. Not allowing enough time for the complete preparation is the most common error.

With all leg placement deriving from the thigh and all circular power enhanced by pushing the thigh in the direction of the turn, the energy created during the preparation is maintained, as the fully extended leg shortens to *retiré* by the time the leg arrives in 2nd position.

The Revolution:

The *port de bras* technique for the *fouetté* differs slightly from that of the standard *pirouette*. At the end of the preparation, the arms are placed in 2nd position to commence the turn. After the body has revolved a 1/4 turn, the left arm has traveled half a circle to join the right arm. They remain together in 5th *en avant* for half a circle, until the left arm arrives at its starting position (2nd) and remains there, while the body and the right arm continue for another quarter turn, ending with the left leg in *demi-plié*, right leg extended in 4th *dégagé* front, and right arm in 5th *en avant*, posed to repeat the preparation.

A common fault during the *fouetté* is unsupported arms, droopy elbows totally lacking practical function, and hands turned with palms downward instead of facing each other. Frequently this arm and hand placement will contract at the elbows, and with each turn the *port de bras* will present a slicing effect, the dancer merely going through the arm motion without creating any momentum.

The proper *port de bras* is the only true source of momentum for the rotation of the torso. The *pirouette* part of the *fouetté* depends on coordinating the working of the right leg from 2nd position into *passé* position, with the incoming left arm and shoulder face increasing the momentum created during the preparation.

All too often, at the point of initiating the *passé*, a dancer will reach backward with the lower part of the leg, rather than placing the leg directly into the *passé* position. (This may very well have been the original intent of the exercise, creating a small *rond de jambé en l'air* while turning — therefore the name "*fouetté*.") Even so, the *fouetté* exercise is far more successful with the leg opening from 4th into 2nd, with the energy continuing inside the thigh and remaining there after placing the leg into *passé*. Attempting to create a *rond de jambé en l'air* at that instant will dissipate the energy created through the preparation.

The *fouetté soutenu* must be performed as thirty-two single turns, rather than by attempting to string them all together as one long, connected blurry whirl.

Spotting:

Spotting is the act of keeping the head (eyes) facing the starting point as long as possible during the first and last stages of the *pirouette*. Focusing with level eyes on the reference point helps to maintain balance. Spotting while revolving prevents dizziness.

Because the torso turns with a rhythm independent of the head, it allows continuous motion while the head remains aligned with its starting position after the turn is initiated, spots, and arrives at the original position before the *pirouette* is completed.

The head remains stationary during the first quarter turn of the torso. When it can no longer remain in its starting position; it is forced into action by the incoming shoulder. The head spins quickly, at a faster rate than the torso, to arrive at its starting position again, spotting over the outgoing shoulder. In the time it takes the head to travel a full revolution the torso has traveled only half a turn.

The end of the spot is not the end of the turn; for the torso, there is still a quarter turn to go. Keep the turn going until both the spot and personal front face in the same direction. The head does not provide the energy for the rotation of the body.

The Horizontal *Pirouette*

The horizontal *pirouette*[1] causes frustration simply because dancers and teachers do not understand the technique for doing it.

During any *pirouette*, it is essential that one remain in conscious control of placement and balance. Yet often dancers will start the horizontal *pirouette* on the basis of hope: hoping they will turn the correct way, hoping they will stay on balance and hoping, as they rush into the final position, that somehow it will all work. That is when instinct takes charge.

As mentioned earlier, instinct seems to dictate pulling instead of pushing. Why that

1   To reiterate: the following techniques are only applicable on the horizontal floor.

happens is unclear. The most obvious example of pulling occurs during the *pirouette* in *arabesque* or *attitude.* It takes the greatest concentration and determination to remain in the correct horizontal placement and not give in to the temptation of pulling from horizontal into vertical.

The first rule to keep in mind is that placement is constant. As earlier emphasized, regardless of what preceded it or will follow, the disposition of the body and limbs is the same. This rule is completely ignored when it comes to horizontal *pirouettes* in *arabesque* or *attitude.* (Never forsake placement for the exercise.)

Since *arabesque* and *attitude* are horizontal positions, with the head placed forward of the balancing point, there can be no spotting while turning in these positions. At the very first spot, the alignment of the arms would be completely disorganized and the position would have no resemblance to the intended one. A frequent instance of the *en dedans attitude pirouette* is: once the *attitude* position is attained, the *pirouette* is spotted, the *en haut* arm will be placed behind the head, the torso will pull up and the dancer is no longer in *attitude.*

There appears also to be constant confusion as to whether an *arabesque* or *attitude* turn is *en dedans* or *en dehors*. In the vertical *pirouette*, when directional energy comes from the shoulder and pelvis on the same side of the body, it is an *en dedans* turn; but when the energy comes from opposite sides of the body, the turn is *en dehors*. This distinction is often misunderstood in *arabesque* or *attitude*. By pulling up into the *retiré* from either of these two positions, it will instantly become clear which it is.

As pointed out above, there can be no spotting in horizontal *pirouettes*. In the vertical position, the head is directly over the balancing point, which allows spotting. But when stationary in *arabesque* or *attitude*, the head is forward of the balancing point, with the upper body counterbalancing the gesture leg. The head and body turn in unison at the same rate. This is such an exercise in discipline that few dancers take the time to master this rather trying technique.

Yet, done correctly, both the *arabesque* and *attitude* become spectacular turns.

En Dedans in 1st *Arabesque:*

The *arabesque* is a troublesome position, especially since such a variety of exercises is performed in this position. The most frequently used *arabesque*, of course, is the 1st *arabesque* (*Cecchetti*).

Since most systems agree on the same pose for 1st *arabesque*, we will limit this discussion to that position.

Surprisingly, the arm position of the 1st *arabesque* lies within the rim of the *port de bras* sphere. One simply stays with the arms and left leg in 2nd position *tendu.* Rotate the right heel 1/4 turn *en dedans*, turn the head, looking over the right shoulder and hand and let the left leg adjust into 4th position *tendu* back.

The arms have not moved from the 2nd position but, since the personal front has changed, are now placed in the 1st *arabesque* position. The right hand is in front and center of the chest. The tendency is to place the hand either in line with, or outside the shoulder, but it is vital that the hand remain centered. The correct position keeps the arm and shoulder

Fig. 16. En Dedans in 1st Arabesque.

locked at the shoulder face, preventing the torso from collapsing. In the *pirouette* it is the weight that is pushed in the direction of the *pirouette*.

The preparation:

Place the arms and legs in 2nd position and face the upstage right corner. The arms and legs are in line with the spatial diagonal, from downstage right to upstage left. Rotate the heel simultaneously a quarter turn; the left heel *en dedans*, the right heel *en dehors*. *Demi-plié* with the left leg so all the weight is on the left and none on the right. The right leg is extended straight back. Place the left arm in 5th *en avant*, turn the head left looking over the shoulder and in line with the left foot. The dancer is now placed in 4th position *croisé*. Often this placement is too shallow and is placed from left to right stage rather than in a convincing diagonal.

With the right leg in 4th back, the pelvis has remained in place and is now parallel with the shoulders, the right arm and leg equally extended as a continuity of the shoulders and pelvis. It is of the utmost importance that the shoulders are an aligned link with the arms. While the arms are placed from front to back, the shoulders instinctively will align from left to right. No *arabesque*, *pirouette* or *penché* will be successful with this directional contradiction.

Since this is an *en dedans* turn, the preparation is incoming energy originating from the right shoulder face, arm, groin and back leg. It is essential to practice the preparation from beginning stance into half-toe *arabesque* stance before practicing the revolve. No arm preparation is needed in the *arabesque* turn.

On the *relevé*, bring the torso forward over the supporting leg. In the regular horizontal *arabesque* position open the left arm from 5th *en avant* to forward elongated position. Turn the hand palm down, keeping the arm aligned with the center of the chest. Do not anticipate by reaching with the left arm ahead of the body or lean in the direction of the preparation, or your will be pulling.

All at one time push the incoming shoulder and arm, pelvis and leg in the direction of the final position of the preparation, i.e., facing stage left on half-toe.

This exercise will teach the placement of the *arabesque* and also the distance required for the preparation before the actual turn begins. Repeat the exercise until the correct *arabesque* balance has been achieved. The preparation

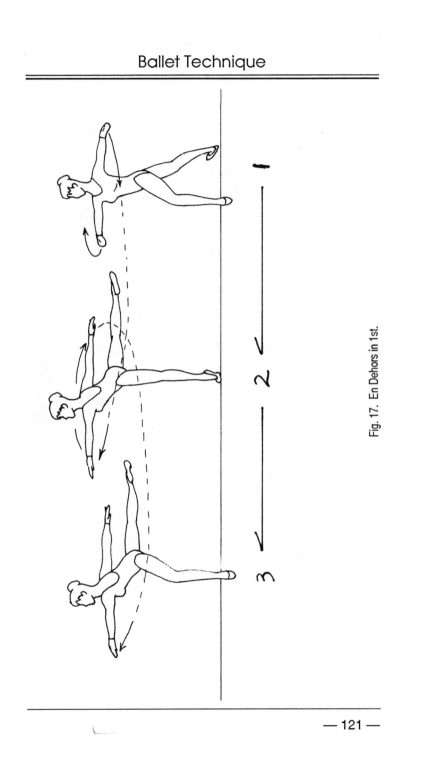

Fig. 17. En Dehors in 1st.

needs 3/8 of a turn before the actual rotation begins. It takes that long to arrive on *relevé*.

When competent in the preparation and balance, apply full push into the turn, from the back shoulder and arm and from the pelvis and leg. The weight must be allowed the full benefit of this preparation, so that the effort of the incoming shoulder and pelvis may bring maximum momentum into the turn. As with all *pirouettes*, accelerate the preparation into the speed of the turn using the whole weight of the body. All too frequently, the preparation is at a faster rate of speed than the *pirouette* and as a consequence, no *pirouette* is possible

A test of discipline is to maintain the correct *arabesque* or *attitude* position during the turn. The incoming arm and leg are parallel, and their joint effort is the correct energy toward a successful *pirouette*.

The placement in horizontal position spreads the weight farther from the axis than in a vertical turn. Hence, *arabesque* and *attitude* turns are executed at a slower speed.

En Dehors Arabesque:

In contrast with the *en dedans arabesque pirouette*, where the preparation is total, with arms, legs and torso weight all working as one with virtually no change from preparation to *pirouette* position, the preparation for the *en dehors pirouette* is divided. The preparation starts from 4th *croisé* facing downstage right. The arms are in 4th. This time the right arm is in 5th front and the left arm is in 2nd.

The preparation starts from downstage right and will end facing stage right. During the *relevé*, the shoulder and arms rotate as one, exchanging arm placement. The left arm comes front and the right arm is placed backward. The back leg rises, pressure is applied in the direction of the turn from the inside of the groin and the incoming shoulder face. While the arms travel a full circle trajectory, with each arm traveling a half, the torso, in *arabesque* position, travels only one-eighth of a revolution before the turn itself begins. Proper counterbalance, with continuous pressure from the incoming shoulder face and outgoing groin, provides reliable energy for the outside *pirouette*.

Once again, it is advisable to practice the preparation until balance and placement are correct. Then, on this firm foundation, add the momentum necessary to create rotation.

Attitude Turns

Remember that the *attitude* is a horizontal position; the torso is forward of the balancing point, in counterbalance with the back leg.

The stationary *attitude* has a helix-like twisting character. The support and directional flow characterizing the *attitude* start from the raised hand in 5th position *en haut,* pass down through the raised arm and in a circular direction across the back, through the Universal Point. They continue down and around the opposite side of the waist, across the front of the pelvis and the open groin, and curve backward through the raised leg.

One can consider this flow as being divided at the waist. There is a forward flow from the waist through the Universal Point and forward and up through the arms. The backward flow starts from tthe same place and passes from the waist across the pelvis and open groin into the leg. The groin is opened to the fullest, with its energy applied in a backward direction. The direction of the arm and shoulder is forward. The leg is supported from the underside of the thigh, which prevents it from dropping out of position.

Support is evenly deployed over the entire torso, arms and legs; the effort and control should not all come from the side of the working arm and leg or, invariably, the whole waist collapses, the back leg no longer remaining behind the body, but closing into 2nd position, with the knee dropping below the foot.

The preparation placement for the *attitude* is the same as for the 1st *arabesque en dedans* turn. Keep the personal front facing downstage right and change the left arm from 4th *en avant* to 2nd, and the right arm from 2nd to 4th *en haut*. Practice the placement of the attitude into *relevé* without the turn. On the *relevé*, the placement of the arms, the leg and the counterbalance must all occur as one. The shoulders must be placed squarely in relation to the head, so that both shoulders are in line with the ears. It is this change of arm placement that provides the momentum for the turn. The preparation must be completed before the turn commences. If not, the shoulder will be left behind, the preparation will lack full power to move the weight, and the arms will not be properly placed.

In the *en dedans attitude pirouette*, incomplete placement of the arms at the end of the *port de bras* is often due to anticipation of the turn itself. This leaves the arm placed back of the shoulder and head, out of the *en haut* peripheral view.

The *port de bras* must be completed, placed in the proper position and in correct relation to the body before the turn commences. Only in the proper position can the arm and shoulder move as one, with the shoulder creating the momentum. Correct complete placement will prevent the chronic error of collapsing at the waist on the side of the incoming arm.

As with the *arabesque*, when timing and balance are mastered the next step is to augment the *relevé* — using the energy of the *port de bras* and the weight of the whole body — to begin an *en dedans pirouette*. Do not pull or lean into the direction of the turn, but push from the shoulder and pelvis of the incoming side.

This exercise can be a bit unnerving at first. After years of spotting in the vertical *pirouette*, suddenly to hold the entire body still and just revolve, at a rather slower pace than in the vertical *pirouette*, takes some getting used to. But it is worth it.

Ballet Technique

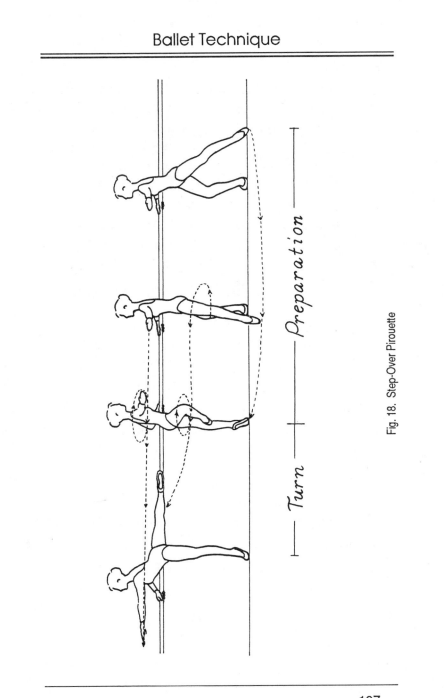

Fig. 18. Step-Over Pirouette

This is how the horizontal *pirouette* works on the horizontal floor. The technique for the raked floor is based on bracing the balance against the rake, straightening the back and placing the arms beyond the peripheral vision. With the arms placed in that position, the shoulder blades contract, the muscle function of the shoulder face is thereby diminished, and much of the available energy is lost. The *attitude* and *arabesque* are thus performed as vertical *pirouettes*, with the usual spotting,

Step-over *Pirouette*

The step-over *piqué pirouette* has a peculiar preparation which is seldom, if ever, done correctly in a class. On stage it is usually done at least partially correctly, but then only during the *adagio* part of a *pas de deux*. Perhaps this is only the result of a choreographic accident. In case this is so, I shall clarify the preparation and turn for those who never get to perform a *pas de deux*.

The best direct exercise for the preparation is at the *barre*. Let us suppose the right hand is placed on the *barre* and the right leg is in front, in *demi-plié*. The left leg is extended back in 4th position *battement soutenu*, and the left arm is extended to the side in 2nd position.

Bring the left leg around with a *rond de jambe a terre en dedans*, until the leg reaches the 2nd position. Then lock the leg at the groin in 2nd. With the leg locked and left arm parallel to the leg, continue the *rond de jambe* with *port de bras* and revolve until the personal front faces the *barre*.

With the leg still in 2nd position, the support leg (right) pushes the left leg onto *piqué* while the torso continues the revolve until facing the opposite direction from the starting direction. The left arm, which has followed the incoming horizontal trajectory, ends with the hand on the *barre*, while the right leg pushes itself in the *retiré* position, the right arm ending simultaneously in 2nd. This preparation requires a half-turn.

The last half of the *rond de jambe* preparation, from 2nd to the final position, makes the difference between this preparation and the one usually practiced on a raked stage.

In most cases the semi-revolution *piqué* is missing from the preparation for the step-over turn. Yet this very preparation, ending facing the opposite direction, is frequently performed during a *pas de deux*. If a turn were initiated, the *port de bras* of the incoming arm and shoulder and the backward push from the thigh into the *retiré* position generates the momentum for the *pirouette*.

A complete *pirouette* would end facing the point at which the preparation ended and the *pirouette* began. To end facing the point where the preparation began would constitute a turn and a half. The push of the second leg, away from the starting point into *piqué retiré* position must be correctly executed in order to make the most of balance and momentum. This preparation has an enormous amount of acceleration and force in its momentum, due to the use of the full length of both legs and the circular *port de bras*. More revolutions than normal are easily attained.

What usually happens in the center (and this stems from the raked stage technique) is that the working leg swings in with a small r*ond de jambe*, ends in *piqué serré* in front of the support leg directly under the weight. The result is that the support leg must be pulled off the floor into *raccourci devant* while pulling the left arm around. It takes a long time to make this technique work, and even then it never looks really good and too often results in a dancer tripping on stage.

On a raked stage this technique may very well be the only workable one. But on a horizontal floor there is no need to modify one's volume of motion. You can step out fully; the horizontal floor does not drop away as the raked floor would.

Stopping the *Pirouette*

It is necessary that a dancer be able to stop a *pirouette* while on one leg (the support leg). The preparation for the turn provides acceleration into the speed of the turn; stopping the *pirouette* uses a similar mechanism to decelerate from the speed of the turn and stop in balance on the support leg.

It is impossible to do this without preparing the stop. The technique of stopping is practiced in sequential action, without initiating the *pirouette*. The gradual rise from the heel that places the foot on half-toe at the beginning of the *pirouette* is reversed. Using guidance from the whole back, especially the back of the leg, roll the foot down until the heel is on the floor.

This lift and roll down control are vital to a successful stop. Having achieved secure control of the *relevé*, the lift from the back and the placement, try a *pirouette*. One *pirouette* can be performed slowly enough to be considered a *relevé en tournant*. Lowering the heel coincides with the end of the spot.

While the spot may be completed, the *pirouette* has still a quarter turn to do before completion. The last spot is the instant where the heel is lowered and the *pirouette* can end on balance. Preparing, turning, and ending with not much momentum makes it possible to practice lower- ing the heel, slowing down the momentum, and sliding into the full stop and final position. This technique applies to stopping all turns, ending on one leg.

Ending the pirouette on half-toe is just a matter of gauging the momentum. A half-toe ending is apt to be more successful with multiple *pirouettes* because the rotating momentum runs out. It is a very exciting ending and an excellent example of balance and placement.

Slowing down the *pirouette* to a complete stop on one leg can also be done with a shift from vertical to horizontal position while still in the *relevé* position. This can be accomplished by a slight extra lift from the revolving heel, which stops the rotation, while simultaneously pushing the heel forward, until the weight settles fully down on the foot again.

The technique of jumping off from the *relevé* to arrest the *pirouette* is an accepted technique. However, the sudden stop does not allow a halt to the momentum and a balanced ending in the required position.

This *pirouette* technique works without fail on the horizontal floor. It would not work on a raked floor. I have observed that all *port de bras* and leg placements for the raked floor are placed as close as possible to the balance axis. The arms are contracted toward the body and the *retiré* leg is placed in the *raccourci* position (foot in front or back of the knee). There is some trajectory, but the arms and legs are pulled immediately toward the center of the balance axis, eliminating the strong centrifugal momentum that would otherwise pull the weight out of alignment toward the down-slope of the rake.

TEACHING BALLET

Good ballet teaching is founded on a thorough knowledge of the craft, combined with a boundless commitment to convey this knowledge. The teacher also needs a passion for the art; this will be recognized by the students and serve to entice them into learning without seeming to do so. Understanding leads to discovery, and discovery is always exciting. Good teaching and eagerly committed students form a productive combination.

There is no routine formula for conducting a class. For any particular technical point, the preparation may be light, or it may be complete, with every exercise and combination structured and planned for that specific goal. It is for the teacher to remain alert to the unexpected, and to be able to incorporate the unforeseen into the structure of the lesson.

There are a number of intangible factors of which the teacher should be aware.

As a rule, dancers endow their teachers with unconditional trust, giving teachers the opportunity to draw the best from their students. If this trust is to be earned, teachers must be absolutely fair, and give the best of themselves to their students.

An experienced teacher will realize that each student is having a "different" class from the other students, and that all students are having a "different" class from the one the teacher is teaching. Students may be executing the steps and combinations requested, yet each one will be concentrating on his or her own technical priorities and on the various secondary components of the exercise, making constant adjustments and improvements. Because of this total concentration and preoccupation, the teacher must at times remind the student of the primary purpose of the exercise. This often happens at the *barre*. It is a not an uncommon experience to be standing nose to nose with a student, who will suddenly snap back to reality, surprised to find the teacher standing there. In all students, this inward concentration tends to obscure outward awareness. They relish such concentration; it provides a sense of privacy and self-reliance, and brings a feeling of accomplishment through focused effort.

As part of that concentration, the student is constantly scanning and examining the body, making corrections and noting the concomitant feelings, which are the basis of comparison for future execution. At the same time, the student must stay with the exercise and music, and must listen to the teacher's instructions.

It often puzzles teachers when a sudden question to the student does not elicit the correct answer. This is not a sign of lack of interest or attention or of lack of knowledge; it is just that the teacher and student have been concentrating on different priorities. That is why it is better not to ask questions. The student can accept interruption of this concentration to receive positive instruction, but to break it for what may seem meaningless questions is absurd. (Dancers show their knowledge in their performance, not in their answers to questions.)

When an error occurs, it is the teacher's responsibility to re-state the correct technical principle. If the problem remains, the teacher must explain it afresh. On the next attempt, the student can apply this information and experience the adjustment. Trust students, when they understand corrections and principles, to do their very best. A teacher should never tire of explaining or repeating the purpose and technical structure of an exercise, but must realize that correct execution does not always come immediately: corrections need repetition, until all the components are understood.

When it is necessary to single out a student for personal correction, the teacher should warn the class that, for emphasis, the error will be exaggerated. To "burlesque" or ridicule a student's mistake is unforgivable; avoid humiliation. It is not always easy to demonstrate a mistake "correctly," but that is no excuse for belittling the student. To demonstrate a mistake, with forewarning and concern, is acceptable. Nothing should be allowed to interfere with the clear purpose of learning. The mind and soul of the student cannot overcome pain inflicted by a thoughtless teacher; for that student, the rest of the class will be a loss. There are too many dancers already who have given up dancing because they could not function under abusive instructors.

It is a rather routine matter to clear up a conventional error, so as to lead the student from mistake to technical mastery. However, it is the unexpected error you have never seen before, or the one which is on the borderline between two different technical principles, which requires true expertise. If you examine all the applicable technical principles, one will emerge as appropriate, and will lead to the answer.

Patience is essential when teaching ballet. Keep corrections short and to the point. Allow time for experimenting with the corrections given. Everyone in the class should know exactly how a correction ought to be applied, although they may not be able to apply it in practice at that time.

Genuine humility is necessary to good teaching. To openly acknowledge one's own mistakes enhances a teacher's authority, rather than diminishing it. And to acknowledge ignorance in some area lends more credence to firmly presented knowledge. When a student asks a question, the teacher must give the correct answer, even if the answer is, "I don't know." If you don't know the answer, say so at once and ask for time to think it over or to look it up. With adequate technical knowledge, the answer will be found. You can then give a full explanation, including the sequence of technical logic by which you arrived at the answer. This will further the student's trust in your artistic and personal integrity.

All teachers at some time have encountered that discouraged and sad-faced student who asks with trembling lips, "What is wrong with me? I don't seem to make any progress." The teacher must be prepared to answer this despair. All of us who studied to become dancers have, from time to time, faced the crisis of apparent lack of progress, and have wondered why. It is a problem that occurs when mastering any craft, and it is particularly acute in ballet. Concentrated study of any subject brings progress in irregular spurts; in ballet these plateaus in learning seem to be more pronounced. The reason may be that all steps incorporate diverse techniques. When all the components are correctly executed, there is successful overall accomplishment. However, if one of the technical components lags in development, the whole exercise will fail. Or a technique may be mastered in one context, yet fail when combined with another technique. It is this imbalance of skill that causes plateau learning. Until all components work correctly, progress is blocked. You can reassure that sad-faced student that progress will come in a sudden thrust, and that patient perseverance in the face of apparent lack of improvement will result in the mastery of all components, and hence in true advancement.

As a teacher, one of your major challenges is yourself. Burn-out, physical and mental fatigue, old injuries that insist on being remembered, too many classes of the same level or different styles, can all contribute to the process of "growing stale." An important factor is the limited material of the profession: ballet has, at best, a limited vocabulary, and in a lower-level class is that much more limited than in an advanced class. Working with that limited material over a long period becomes very trying. To remain energetic, interested, patient, enthusiastic and creative demands constant discipline from the teacher. Few ballet teachers had to deal with such monotonous routine in their careers as professional dancers. Repetition is not creatively stimulating, yet performers on Broadway must face this repetition every night, twice on Wednesdays and Saturdays, for months and sometimes years. They must perform with energy, enthusiasm and honesty from opening night to closing night. Each audience is for them the first audience and each night is opening night.

The teacher must have that same commitment and constancy, whereby every class is a new experience, and every student is seen as if for the very first time. Manipulation of the vocabulary, creating new combinations with the same steps, and providing a constant challenge to body control will preserve the students' interest and keep the teacher alive and fresh. The technical purpose will provide the appropriate step or combination of exercises. This is the way to progress beyond the average.

The teacher creates the atmosphere of the class. Mutual respect and trust provide for easy communication, and allow the teacher to be in charge of any situation. Charisma and fame are qualities that may stand a teacher in good stead, but they are not needed for good teaching. Good teaching technique requires thorough knowledge of the subject, genuine interest in the students' progress, patience and friendly good humor. The teacher-student relationship should be objective, equitable and free of any personal behavior not related to teaching and learning. When you work with a mind free of anxiety, it provides a relaxed, safe atmosphere in which observation and reasoning are more penetrating, progress is faster and communication equal on both sides.

Most students have quite vivid mental pictures of what ballet is all about. These differ from one student to the next, but each student must be gently disengaged from all concepts of the dance not grounded in actual ballet technique. It is frequently believed, for instance, that unless every muscle is active at every moment, something is amiss. The result is a rigid posture.

This needless waste of energy can be seen in a pointed *tendu* foot which refuses to flex upon returning to 1st or 5th, and consequently arrives with a bridged sole. Or one may see flexed wrists, contracted elbows, a raised chest or chin or other affectations. Such reactions are easily observed and simple to correct.

THE CLASS:

Traditionally, a class is divided into two major sections: the *barre* and the center. This division is made in both beginner and professional classes. Each section is in turn sub-divided.

As a rule, beginner classes are one hour in length, while advanced and professional classes last one and one-half hours. The time is apportioned as follows:

Beginners:

»	*Barre*	1/2 hour
»	Center	1/2 hour
»	*Adagio*	10 minutes
»	*Allegro*	10 minutes
»	*Moderato*	10 minutes

Intermediate-Advanced:

- » *Barre*   1/2 hour
- » Center   1 hour
- » *Adagio*   10 minutes
- » *Pirouettes*   10 minutes
- » *Allegro*   10 minutes
- » *Adagio*   10 minutes
- » *Moderato*   10 minutes

During the *barre* exercises, you should integrate or emphasize a particular difficulty which will be developed during the center work.

The *Barre*:

During the student's formative stage, the *barre* is a support and balance substitute while positions and directions — in the main, rather than static — are introduced. The student can concentrate on the execution of the new material while the *barre* provides support. Once these standard materials have been mastered, the *barre* work does not vary much from the prior purpose: all placements and exercises are reviewed, as reminders to the body. *Barre* work also serves as a warm-up in preparation for the center work. The more variation there is in vocabulary, as well as in directions and levels of leg and body placement, the better the student is prepared for the center work.

Plié:

The *plié* is by tradition the first exercise at the *barre*. It is a very complete and practical exercise, providing practice in turn-out, strengthening the thighs, lengthening the calf muscles, practicing the neutrality of the toes and the pushing technique of the heels.

The sequence of positions for *pliés* is variable; however, the 2nd position is the least stressful on the turn-out and is therefore ideal as starting position for *pliés*. 1st position should come next, followed by 4th, and ending the *plié* series with 5th position. The 3rd position, although still used, is frequently eliminated from the *plié* exercises.

One can progress from *demi-plié* to *grand plié*, and elaborate the sequence with *cambrés* and *port de bras* for placement. One may end with *relevés*, checking for relaxation, turn-out and balance.

The transition from one *plié* position to the next introduces the *tendu*. After the *pliés* at the *barre*, a good plan is to work the leg from lower, through middle, to higher level, gradually, with a variety of *tempi* in isolation and balance exercises.

Tendu:

The next exercise is the *tendu*. Its major purpose is the directional placement of the leg in 4th front, 2nd and 4th back, with precise manipulation of the pelvis and the brushing of the foot out and in. (I shall no longer refer to the turn-out, since it is included in all ballet positions.)

The most common mistake with the *tendu* is the lack of downward pressure from the foot against the floor on the way out. This results in the foot leaving the floor just before completing the *tendu*. The same applies in returning the foot. If the student anticipates closing to the starting position, pressure is taken off the floor and the foot returns without floor contact. Downward pressure has to be maintained in both directions.

Also, one must be aware of the correct working of the foot during the *tendu*. The toes must travel the toeline. The toeline is an imaginary straight line starting at the toe in 5th or 1st position and ending with the final position of the toe in *tendu*. Only thus is the heel allowed to rise and lower into a pointed foot. If the toes flip toward the heel, the foot is pointed from the toes, negating the proper technique for pointing the foot.

To develop foot awareness, place the foot in *tendu* position, push the body toward the extended foot, thereby lowering the heel. From this placement in 4th or 2nd, push the body back on the support leg from the working foot, ending in the original *tendu*. This exercise develops an awareness of moving the body as one, and of pushing away from the starting point.

The same exercise can be enhanced by adding a *demi-plié*, *relevé*, *demi-plié*, and returning the body onto the support leg, closing the working leg in 5th and adding an extra *tendu* to fill out the count. A good exercise is the *temps lié*, which furthers understanding of the transfer of weight from starting to arrival point.

The *tendu* is the beginning and end of many steps. It therefore requires the strictest attention.

Dégagé:

The *dégagé* is an extension of the *tendu*. The leg passes through the *tendu* position before it rises off the floor and becomes the *dégagé*. It is also the first exercise in which the leg leaves the floor, and it introduces to the class the precise height of the leg, the energy controlling the outward thrust, the arrest and lowering of the leg, using the groin muscles.

Here, too, the primary directions are to be precisely executed. One may incorporate *relevés*, *battement cloche*, *port de bras en dedans* and *en dehors*, flexing and pointing the foot, and *rond de jambe* at *dégagé* height. It is up to the teacher to enrich this basic exercise with variations that are relevant to the purpose of the *dégagé*.

At this stage of the class, tradition ends and the teacher's preference takes over. One may, for instance, move to a recapitulation of the *tendu* and *dégagé* combined, keeping in mind that the height of the leg must increase, and that the brushing and rolling action of the foot must be practiced.

Battement Soutenu:

Again, this is an appropriate exercise for practicing the articulation of the foot, the *demi-plié* and the turn-out of the second leg. In addition, the head inclination can be trained in harmony with the *port de bras*. One can repeat this exercise, placing the working leg into *dégagé*.

Battement Piqué:

Except for starting and ending, the effort for the *piqué* originates from the groin, with the whole leg working as one. At first, it can be performed at a slow tempo to establish the correct use of the technique. Yet, the correctness of the *battement piqué* must be verified by increasing the tempo. Invariably, with this increase the effort tends to transfer to the foot and presents a tapping effect rather than remaining a true *battement.* Introduce a combination of *dégagé-piqué* as a reminder that *dégagé* and piqué are of the same height

Rond de Jambe:

The *rond de jambe* can be practiced *à terre* and at *dégagé* height, with *port de bras en dedans* and *en dehors*. It can be completed by *chassé* into *arabesque allongé* from the *en dehors* or *en dedans rond de jambe, chassé* backward, ending in *demi-plié*, with the working leg raised in 4th front and the arm in *effacé* position.

Retiré:

Retiré emphasizes the rolling up and down of the foot and the articulation of the knee. It is important, as well, to practice placing the tip of the working foot against the inside of the support leg knee. The *retiré* is the neutral position. *Raccourci* places the foot in *retiré* with the foot either in front or in back of the knee.

Another exercise for articulation of the knee and foot is the *balloné* with accent in. Or students can practice placing the working foot at the correct *sur le coup de pied* position, *frappé*, accent out, at slow and fast tempo. Tempo, full *retiré* height and basic directions are all used, and when mastered, the diagonal directions should be added.

Fondu:

Fondu with *dévelopé* at *dégagé* height or at full height in *effacé* or *écarté* including *arabesque*. The *dévelopés* can end with the whole of the support foot on the floor or in *relevé*. The *fondu dévelopé* can end in *tendu* or *dégagé* alternating front and back, with a *petit battement sur le coup de pied* as the link between front and back.

Frappé:

The *frappé* provides articulation of the foot on its own, without use of the floor or displacement of the weight. It also practices articulation of the knee and the repeated placing of the thigh in 2nd with the return of the foot in *sur le coup de pied* position. To further the articulation of the foot and knee, add *retiré* exercises and *petit battement sur le coup de pied* combinations. The arms can practice the momentum for rotation.

Some examples:

» Three *frappés* front. On the fourth *frappé*, *relevé* with a half-turn *en dedans*. The working leg is now placed *sur le coup de pied* back of the support leg.

» Three *frappés* back, with *relevé*, with a turn *en dehors*, bringing the working leg in front *sur le coup de pied* of the support leg.

» Four *frappés* in 2nd, and end the exercise with four counts of *petit battements soutenus*.

» Then repeat the whole exercise, starting with *frappé* back.

All articulation has now been sufficiently practiced. It is time to develop strength, and raise the exercise to a higher level.

Dévelopé:

As we have seen, the *dévelopé* can commence from the *fondu:* now it must be employed from the *retiré* position. From the *retiré*, the leg is raised through the *attitude*, into an extended leg. The leg can be held while the student lets go of the *barre*. All directions need to be practiced with and without *relevé*.

Here, as in all backward placements of the leg, the pelvis pivots back with the extended leg in *attitude* or *arabesque*. The same applies in slow *rond de jambe en dehors* or *en dedans* with extended leg, or in *attitude*. It is essential to keep the leg at the same height. The *dévelopé* can be preceded by *pas de cheval*, ending in *relevé* and balance, with the working leg held in the extended position.

Cambré toward the extended leg, front and back:

This exercise strengthens the support, while isolating the *cambré* from the support leg.

Having finished with the strength exercise, it is wise to increase the tempo, but with a less strenuous exercise such as:

- » *Flic-flac* with or without the *en tournant.*

- » *Petits battements serrés* with *port de bras en dehors* and *en dedans.*

- » Double or triple *petits battements sur le coup de pied.*

(Personally, I tell my students I expect all the *sur le coup de pied* positions, either in place or turning, to contact the support leg. This contact assures the student that the leg is properly placed and not in "limbo.")

Adagio:

The *adagio* need not be longer than the strength exercise. However, it must be composed of more varied positions and techniques. Horizontal and vertical balance, inside and outside *fouetté* turns, *arabesque allongé*, and *piqué arabesque* can all be included in the *adagio*.

Rond de Jambe en l'Air:

This can be initiated from *dévelopé à la seconde* or from *fondu dévelopé la seconde*. The *rond de jambe* can either be done with the whole of the supporting foot on the floor, or from half-toe. It can also be started at half height, always making certain that the foot describes a complete oval, by touching the inside of the knee or calf of the support leg, and with a complete extension of the working leg into 2nd position. *Balloné* can be part of the *rond de jambe* exercise, emphasizing the incoming accent of the *balloné*, and the outgoing accent of the *rond de jambe.*

Grand Battement:

By tradition, *grand battement* is the last exercise at the *barre*. It offers the leg the opportunity to use full momentum in all the corporal or diagonal directions. The *grand battement* can be enhanced with *grand battement piqué*, from *tendu* or the *serré* position. This may include *dévelopé* at full height.

All the aforementioned and following exercises are suggestions for a sequence of *barre* work in preparation for the center. They can be changed or elaborated infinitely by the teacher, depending on the technical plan of the class.

Some teachers prefer to conclude *barre* work with stretches.

First 10 Minutes

Without the balancing aid provided by the *barre*, the student must now depend on personal balance control and isolation of effort. With beginners, the first 10 minutes of the center should be a recapitulation of the *barre* exercises just completed. The challenge of balance through *grand plié* from 1st, and later from 5th position, allows the student to experience the correct use of the Universal Point. These *pliés* can be extended to *relevé* and held on half-toe. The *tendu* and *dégagé* can be repeated with spatial variation through *croisé*, front and back, and *effacé* front and back, completing the exercise with the appropriate *port de bras.*

Promenade:

Although the *promenade* is not an easy exercise, it contains a vital array of techniques necessary for the student to master. The sooner it is introduced, the more benefit to the student. It is primarily an application of free-standing balance in which the initiative originates from the heel. If the effort originates from the torso, the promenade will have a "hula" effect. Pivot must be on the ball of the foot, not the heel.

The gesture leg in the turn-out position, can be placed s*ur le coup de pied*, in back of the support leg, or in the *retiré* position. The energy follow-through comes from the incoming shoulder. The same positions are ideal for introducing the rolling up and down from the heel of the support leg and balance on the half toe. It must be stressed that the success of balance depends on placement and absolute immobility of the entire body.

Rond de Jambe:

The *rond de jambe à terre* and at *dégagé* height, *en dehors* and *en dedans*, is a challenge to the isolated working of the leg and the proper adjustment of the torso from vertical to horizontal while retaining balance.

In general:

The object of these first 10 minutes of center work is to provide primary exercises for the isolated working of the leg in a static position.

The second 10 minutes of the center should be devoted to a transfer of the weight, starting at one point and arriving at another. An appropriate exercise, which includes balance, transfer and articulation of the heel, is *tendu la seconde*, *relevé* from the support foot, and transfer of weight onto the gesture leg, rolling down from the heel and ending with what was the support leg in *tendu* position, closing in 1st or 5th.

Keep in mind that the thrust of the *relevé* is directed upward rather than toward the extended foot. Beginners are bound to fail in attempting this exercise to the front or back. The reason is that, with the back leg extended by the pelvis, the transfer from back to front will make the back leg too long to match the forward *tendu* leg. This makes the student very uncomfortable. Similarly, ingoing from front to back, since the pelvis is extended with the leg, the front leg has to be pulled in from the groin. This contradicts the never-pull-always-push principle, but in this instance there is no technically correct substitute.

The *glissade* provides an even clearer example of weight transfer. The *chassé* and *temps lié* in all directions both transfer the weight. Transfer of weight in variable directions provides a good basis for the use of relevant exercises.

The last 10 minutes are devoted to exercises in the higher level. The *changement de pieds* is by its very simplicity ideal for introducing the jump. This exercise is undemanding, yet it familiarizes the student with pushing off from both legs and landing on both legs. The student learns to thrust and absorb the weight. Some adult beginners find this simple exercise somewhat frightening but that fear is quickly overcome.

The simple *jeté* is perhaps most often practiced as the first elevation step. It is a simple action, and one which most young girls have already used in games such as "hopscotch." The same applies to the *jeté temps levé*.

The sooner *assemblé* and *sissonne* are introduced, the sooner the student will come to understand their complete technical opposition. In the *assemblé*, one starts from one leg and lands on both, taking off and landing in the same place. The *sissonne* starts from both legs at the same time and ends on one leg; in it one travels from the starting point to a separate, predetermined arrival point. These exercises can cause quite a bit of confusion, but a very important technical understanding is achieved in appreciation of the difference between the two.

Another step in center work, one often introduced early, is the *pas de chat*. This is a horizontal traveling step; hence one can utilize the spatial diagonal. The fact that this step is introduced early does not mean that it is an easy step. During the *pas de chat*, the weight remains over the starting leg from the moment the *retiré* is initiated, through the transfer with elevation, until landing on balance on the initiating leg.

In distinction to the *pas de chat*, the *glissade* keeps the weight on the support leg after the *dégagé* has taken place. The weight will be transferred the moment the support leg pushes the weight towards the arrival point, on what was the starting leg. In the *glissade*, the weight is transferred from one leg onto the other, while in the *pas de chat* it remains over the initiating leg from start to finish. The *pas de chat* shares an interesting characteristic with the *pas de basque* and the *gargoulliade*: in each of them it is the thigh which initiates the spatial distance and direction.

An appropriate ending for a beginner class is to place the arms in the principal positions. The arms and their placement can be understood and executed by the most elementary student. The placement can be performed without lengthy instruction and practice. There is as yet no universally accepted *port de bras*. Various systems utilize different versions, to suit their techniques or aesthetic concepts.

The following arm positions are the most suitable for practical participation of the arms:

» 2nd position.

» 5th - *en bas, en avant, en haut.*

» 4th - *en bas, en avant, en haut.*

ADVANCED CLASSES:

The structure of intermediate, advanced and professional classes is similar to that of a beginner class. The *barre* work should progress in the same gradual fashion, but whereas beginners learn new steps and positions, advanced and professional classes practice more complicated combinations. Nevertheless, the purpose of the *barre* is still to provide a warm-up and an application of all techniques. A well-planned *barre* period need not be longer than half an hour.

The center work must be the challenging portion of the class. The combinations should encompass as much of the vocabulary as possible to prevent overlooking any technical principles.

Center Work:

The First Half Hour

Adagio: (10 minutes)

Start with a short exercise, the content of which might be something that may not have been covered at the *barre*. This exercise is followed by the *adagio*, which need be no longer than sixteen bars. In this way the student can concentrate on the technical difficulty, rather than trying to remember a longer combination or watching the other students for cues. The purpose of the *adagio* is balance with continuous, sustained motion throughout the exercise. Some typical steps available for the *adagio* are:

» *Fouetté* from *dévelopé* 4th front into *arabesque* or *arabesque penché*.

» *Dévelopés*.

» Slow *pirouettes* ending in a balance pose.

» *Cambré* front and back.

» *Tombés* and *piqués* in *attitude* or *arabesque.*

Pirouette: (10 minutes)

Variations on the *pirouette* are legion, and it is imperative that a *pirouette* segment be included in each class; instruction in the many variations will require several classes. Both *en dehors* and *en dedans* directions must be included, though not necessarily in the same *pirouette*, but it is vital that both directions receive attention. The class should include at least three different kinds of *pirouette*. These can start from different preparations, and can end on one or both legs, in the starting direction or in another direction.

Allegro: (10 minutes)

The *allegro* can be a stumbling block for many dancers. While the *adagio* and the *pirouette* are not affected by the dancer's height and weight, in *allegro* the shorter, lighter student has an advantage, since the object is agility and tempo. The teacher will do well to divide the class into groups according to stature, and then slow the tempo slightly for the taller, heavier group. (The taller students will get their chance to shine in the elevation combinations.)

Basic *allegro* steps are *assemblés battu, petit jeté battu, brisé, pas de chat, pas de bourrée dessus* and *dessous, temps de cuisse,* etc. There are too many available steps to present the full list here. Typical are small jumps and small steps which keep the working legs and feet directly under the body, but use the full length of the leg and displacement of the weight. The aim is to practice facility at a rapid pace. The steps should include directional changes and articulation, from the lower level to upper level. Directions can be varied with front, back, side and diagonal exercises which call for speed without a great deal of elevation.

Remember, it is not that the steps are difficult; it is tempo, demanding fast thinking and moving, that make it seem the steps are difficult.

The Last Half Hour:

This period is devoted to space-covering steps and exercises requiring a greater degree of skill and dexterity. The following progression of combinations is from *adagio*, through *allegro*, to *marcato*. These exercises are designed to cover distance and elevation, with as much variety of ballet vocabulary as possible. The body is already warmed up and has been led through all the technical principles. It is now ready to meet more demanding challenges.

All steps and combinations should test the limits of the student. This is, in fact, the part of the class to which most dancers look forward, the time when class takes on a freer, more "dancy" quality. Aware of this, the wise teacher will have in mind the intended technical challenge of the exercises or combinations to be utilized. Beautiful and "dancy" combinations are great fun for the dancers, but if the intention is solely for this quality, and not for technical mastery, it is a waste of time.

Adagio: (10 Minutes)

The first 10 minutes are devoted to combinations in a moderately slow tempo. The intent here is the constant progression of the exercise. During these combinations, which are usually based on the diagonal, it is vital that the distance be covered. The teacher must say how many repetitions of the combination are required to fill the diagonal.

Here, as with all combinations, establishing the spatial direction does not preclude the teacher's including personal directions contrary to the spatial direction. Thus, if the spatial direction is from upstage left to downstage right, students might, at some point in the combination, find their personal fronts facing downstage left.

The whole of the ballet vocabulary is available for combinations at this tempo and with these directions. Technical intent will determine the teacher's choice of steps. The level of technical difficulty must be set to suit the respective abilities of intermediate and advanced students.

Allegro: **(10 Minutes)**

The second 10-minute segment emphasizes the progressive *allegro*, which requires a precision frequently overlooked by the student. 5th position becomes 4th, personal front changes to spatial front or downstage, horizontal steps change to vertical, and the directional progress may be stifled.

The teacher must be alert to such failings, and must discipline students toward conscious accuracy. Faults are the result of unmastered continuous spatial progress, combined with the tempo and the challenge of the exercise.

The *allegro* should include steps executed in one manner by females and in another by males. *Brisé battu* can become brisé *volé*; *pirouette* can become *tours en l'air. Emboité* followed by *fouettés* can be substituted for *grand pirouette.* Both can end with multiple *pirouettes,* perhaps *gargoulliade* for the women and *jeté passé* for the men. All the steps that can be performed with *battu* should be included. Articulation, continuity, *ballon,* brilliance and accuracy are the essence of the *allegro*; the desired accomplishment of this segment is swiftness.

Moderato: (10 Minutes)

The final 10 minute segment is reserved for all aerial steps and combinations based on elevation and covering distance in the high level. There is a host of suitable steps:

> » *Cabriole battu,* front and back.

> » *Grand jeté en tournant battu.*

» Double *saut de basque en dehors* and *en dedans.*

» *Rivoltade.*

» *Tour en l'air* in *attitude* or *la seconde,* varying the landing to be on both legs, or on one, or on the knee.

As in the *allegro,* the tempo can be adjusted for male or female dancers. Elevation is the object, and the tempo should encourage maximum effort. The combinations are designed to traverse the diagonal, but the *manége* is frequently used by males and females in classical variations, so that pattern should be made familiar by occasionally using it in this segment.

The same holds true for *fouetté soutenu* (women) and *grand pirouette* (men), with *relevé* at each revolution, or with *sauté* from *demi-plié* ending with multiple *pirouettes.*

The class can end with *port de bras* or *révérence.*

As an economical and practical convention for communication with the student, it is a good idea to divide the body into sections. The torso is one unit; the functioning of the upper arms in conjunction with the torso, or the isolated working of the arms for correct placement independent of the torso is another. Similarly for the thighs: on the one hand, independent working and placement, and on the other, working as a unit with the torso. When it is realized that the upper section of the limbs does all the placing, then the lower parts, when unified with the upper, will work as one in the desired position. The feet are insular — they have their own practice. However, released from the body's weight, they unite with the lower section of the leg.

There should be as little mention as possible of the muscular system, analysis of which results in too much abstract explanation. It is easier to understand placement when it is explained in terms of the subdivided body sections. The muscles then automatically come into action. The upper part of a limb is a tangible, visible unit; it can be observed and corrected without ambiguity. It should be possible to give all instructions in terms of technical principles and body sections. You should talk about the technical principles themselves: talk ing about pearls, water, opening and closing doors, glass plates and the like has no place in the communication of ballet technique. Communication must be professional or it is worthless.

In the early years of ballet study, new steps were continually introduced. True, there are steps so difficult that only exceptional dancers are capable of performing them. However, for most dancers there comes an end to what they can achieve.

Once arrived at that stage, most of the vocabulary becomes repetitious. This very repetition can supply an exciting challenge for the teacher. Once all the steps are known, the teacher has unlimited scope for devising combinations to focus on the purpose of the class. This is particularly so at the *barre*. In this way, familiar material becomes fresh and the students remain alert and challenged.

Combinations should be kept short. This has a great advantage, in that the student can concentrate on technical application, allowing the exercise to be repeated more often. The justification for long exercises is that they train the memory. But this is the role of rehearsal: in class, we are concerned with the mastery of technique. When the dancer comes to rehearsal, any lack of quick memory will be more than compensated by better technical execution.

Ballet training in the USA is, as a rule, inadequate. Good teaching and poor teaching alike are delivered with equal sincerity, and with full belief that the instructions are correct and in the best interest of the student. Teachers in the USA are mainly self-taught; they have discovered from their own personal experiences the teaching techniques they use.

It would be a tremendous help if aspiring ballet teachers could spend time studying the principles of ballet and the techniques of teaching. This would give teachers and students confidence in their mutual efforts.

Some teachers have discarded the traditional system for systems derived from their own experience. Not surprisingly, they nearly all say the same thing. But they do not have a central theory on which to base their findings. Even though they discover a new logic, some of the old technique may still be a part of the whole and may work against the new formulations. Lack of a central theory makes their explanations contradictory and inconclusive. They have not thought back towards the purpose of the step and its relation to others of the same technical character. They have not compared their theory of one step with their theory of another, so as to arrive at a comprehensive theory.

I am convinced that, with clarification, these teachers will discover what they already knew but could not formulate. It could well be that these findings, logical and practical, could some day become a universal system for all horizontal floor technique.